A RANT TOO

First published 2008

© 2008 Fraser Blake

This edition published by Fraser Blake and Kevin Bryan 2008

ISBN 978-1-84651-991-8

To Jean
with best wishes

Fraser Bloke

Dedicated to my wife, Annie

ACKNOWLEGEMENTS

On writing this book I really need to thank the many friends who offered me anecdotes and, above all, encouragement to stay the course and complete the job. Help that I asked for was always generously and freely given with offers for more if needed. Above all, the encouragement and support received from my family was supreme.

Cover design by Tim Blake tim@timblake.com

About the Author

Fraser Blake was born in Johannesburg, South Africa but left there as a baby and was brought up in Eritrea until the age of 11 when he was sent to boarding school in Scotland. There he attended a couple of minor public schools until he was 18. Neither school was a great success when it came to learning or career advice and he left with no clue as to what he might do for a career. His father suggested he join the B.S.A. Police in Rhodesia. He felt this would help to 'mature' him. So he joined the force in 1962.

In 1965 Ian Smith declared independence and he felt it was time to leave. A state of emergency had been declared so he had to find a roundabout rout out of the police as no officers were being released. He did this by joining the immigration service. Inter governmental changes were allowed. It was much easier to resign from this department after the minimum service period of 1 year. So he was an Immigration Officer for a year at the end of which he resigned and returned to Britain. The idea was to further his education. He had left school with only four 'O' levels so he had to attend night school to study for more exams.

In Manchester he was offered a job with the Ministry of Employment. Whilst working there finding work for the unemployed, a job came in from a brand new shop called Mothercare. This was for a storeman/driver and the wage offered was nearly double what he was getting as a lowly civil servant. He applied and got the job. He worked there for the following 9 months when he achieved the necessary exams to gain entry to St. John's College in York, to train as a teacher. After the 3 year course he received a Teacher's Certificate and then went on to complete a B.Ed. (Hons) degree at Leeds University. He taught at Danesmead Secondary Modern School in York for a year when a very attractive job in Saudi Arabia was advertised in a Sunday paper. The attractive part was that it more than doubled his salary again. In 1974 he took a very rapid commercial TEFL course and applied and was offered the job.

In September 1974 he went to teach English in Jeddah, Saudi Arabia for three years. Here, he very quickly learned to speak Arabic whilst his young Arab charges, in common with many children learning a foreign language, paid scant attention to their English lessons. At the end of his third year he was head hunted by a building company because of his ability to speak Arabic. Returning to England in 1978 he bought, along with a partner, a small printing works which he managed for about ten years. At the same time he had a share in a North Yorkshire pub for a couple of years.

In 1990 he decided to change his life again and went to try his luck selling houses in France where he has been ever since. He enjoys reading, writing and wine tasting in small privately owned vineyards.

Definition in Webster's Encyclopaedic Dictionary of the English Language

rant 1. *v.i.* to use bombastic language, esp. in public speaking, [of an actor] to be declamatory in a ludicrously exaggerated way, to be noisily angry, *v.t.* to utter with exaggerated emphasis 2. *n.* a piece of ranting [obs. Du. *randten*, to rave]

CONTENTS

RANT 1: ON RELIGION

The most important thing about religion and a point most people like to forget, or even deny, is that it is man-made. In general the gods of old were seen or could be seen, they were either statues or stones or obelisks, or objects like the sun or the moon or even a mountain. The Jews were probably the first nation to come up with a totally unseen god. This was a very good idea for the rulers and priests as it relied on faith and could not be disproved, nor proved for that matter. Christianity and then Islam followed the same route and the same god although this would be difficult to recognise from the interaction between the three religions ever since. All the creators of the main religions have been men, as in Jesus, Mohammed, Buddha, Confucius, and most of the prophets of the Old Testament were also men although there were one or two women. They all claimed direct lines to God but at the end of the day they were men and during their lives were just seen as such. Like all men, they were born of a mother and a father in the normal way, lived a life and died as do all humans. During their lives they may have become great leaders or sometimes were shunned as were many of the prophets of old but they all backed their leadership with 'words from god'. However, not until after their deaths did any of their followers ever succeed in getting the same line. God only speaks to those who want to hear and if you want to hear that badly then no doubt you will. None were deified during their lifetime, rather this was an honour accorded them long after their deaths. There has never ever been a single provable instance throughout history of God - any god - revealing itself to man - any man or woman, or even talking to anyone. It is always a person on his or her own who hears the voice or sees the vision and never a group of people. Also, apart from Adam who never actually existed, it is never god but one of his closest helpers, as in an angel. Many men

3

and fewer women claim that they are in direct communication or that they speak to God but this is easily said and no doubt some of them genuinely believe it. What we [that is mankind in general] have not come anywhere near understanding yet is the power and intricacies of the human mind. You can think yourself into anything so why not a message from heaven or god? There are those who use the word of god to their own disreputable ends and often seem to get a following. The general public can be a very gullible lot and many of these preachers, holy men, gurus, call them what you like, became very rich off the pickings of their followers. For example, Joseph Smith of the Mormons, L. Ron Hubbard and his Scientology, and Sun Myung Moon and his Unification Church, to name but a few. These three alone can count their followers in millions and there is always a monetary element to their following. The faithful have to give a certain percentage or all of their money to the movement. The Maharishi Mahesh Yogi is another example. He was leader of the Spiritual Regeneration Movement and managed to attract many celebrities among his followers and actually had a fleet of Rolls Royces at his disposal. Then there are the real baddies such as Jim Jones, sometimes called 'the Reverend'. He was another leader who managed to con people into following him. Although his followers numbered fewer than a thousand it is very difficult to understand how such a man, who was obviously mentally unstable, could attract even that many believers. When he fell foul of the authorities in San Francisco he decided to set up home in Guyana, on the north east coast of South America, and was followed by his faithful. When on the point of being exposed as a charlatan by a US senator, he killed him and also some journalists, and then managed to persuade most of his followers to commit suicide. Those that were not so keen were shot. How do these people manage to con so many?

4

Priests, mullahs, monks and holy men and women in general are good at convincing people that they speak with the authority of god. But, in actual fact, it is the authority of learning. That is why they have to go to university and pass exams so that when questioned they can answer sensibly and with some authority. Or they see images or have visions to back up what they want to get across. It does seem odd that many intelligent people who in normal everyday life can be relatively sceptical about so many things can be taken in so easily by religion. Tradition and, of course, education play a big part. However, it is certain that the human ego has a lot to answer for here. So great is the ego that mankind cannot possibly believe that there is nothing after death. The eternal questions keep rearing their ugly heads - why do we exist, how did we come to exist and if this life is all, is it worth it? Religion is based on the fact that above all else we hope that there is something after death and because life is such a struggle that it will be a lot easier. In fact this is what all religions offer, a life after death that will be a lot easier and happier as long as you behave yourself on earth.

If logic is applied to religion it just does not work. Religion requires bountiful amounts of blind faith. Believe because that is what I say, so argue the religious, and if you don't believe me then it has been written down. The holy books tell it all. Because it is in a book it is right. But all the holy books ever written have nothing to do with the hand of god and everything to do with the hand of man. The prophets who wrote the holy books all maintained that theirs were the 'words of God'; - well they would, wouldn't they? Looked at logically how is this possible? In fact the notion is ludicrous, yet they are all taken seriously and believed by a lot of people. However, if one of them was fibbing why not all, which is equally feasible? It is argued, for example, that the words of Christ and Mohammed came from god and, as it happens, the same god. They can't both be right, can they? But millions of people believe they are. But they could equally both be wrong and there are millions of people who really believe this too, but it's just not fashionable to say so. The most ridiculous thing is that both these huge religions believe in the same god and their followers have killed each other by the thousands through the millennia. So if one is right and the other wrong then we can surmise that god himself has made it impossible to choose. And what about all the other religions that flourish, are they all wrong too, or could any one of these be the right one? Another problem here is that every religion along with its followers, believes it is the only authentic one and is therefore the only one that can possibly be genuine, so there is no room for manoeuvre.

The very thought of a god as a being who created everything is totally inexplicable because then we need a creator who created that being. If god just 'happened' then why not mankind and everything else? We cannot really have it both ways. If we need a god to bring us into being then really we need an explanation as to how god came into being in the first place. If god just happened then we could apply the same logic to our own appearance. The very thought of an all-powerful entity just coming into being and then having the power or ability to create, and create something as big and complicated as the universe let alone the sheer complexity that exists on earth, is really unsustainable. Furthermore, if it has happened once why should it not happen again? Another rival god would be a bit of fun, as they would probably end up fighting as humans do and presumably that would be Armageddon. If you put your mind to it and really try to fathom out GOD, the mental gymnastics that are involved create total exhaustion and, of course, you would come to the conclusion that logically a god cannot actually exist. This is probably why most of the greatest thinkers and intellectuals throughout the ages never really believed in a god. In the end, it is actually easier to believe in the Big Bang theory of creation and the mixture of resultant chemicals which brought life into being, than it

6

is in god. Big Bang is possible and has almost been proven, God is impossible to explain and can never be. To believe in god requires blind faith and no thought, logic or questioning which is why all the great religions indoctrinate their children from the earliest possible age. It is notable that when many of the top scientists talk about the beginning of the universe they never mention god. It can also be argued that throughout the ages many great men such as philosophers, politicians, generals and even churchmen, including Popes, have actually shown scant regard for the notion of or belief in god. Niccolo Machiavelli summed it up well with his last words, 'I desire to go to hell and not to heaven. In the former place I shall enjoy the company of Popes, kings and princes while in the latter are only beggars, monks and apostles.' He was here verbalising what most high society of the time felt but could not actually say for that would have been blasphemy or heresy and in those days people were burned for either. However, if Machiavelli thought that most of the top echelons of society at the time did not believe in being good enough to go to heaven then it may be concluded that they did not believe it really existed. Furthermore, a brief look at the writings and beliefs of most philosophers will show that few, if any, really believed in god. One or two of the early ones such as Leibniz tried hard to explain god but then usually ended up tying themselves in knots and becoming the laughing stock of their contemporaries.

A justification for religion is that it is needed as a control. A quick look at all religions shows that broadly speaking they tell the same story – be good, obey the laws of the land, look after each other, do not steal, do not kill etc. etc., and there will be a reward in the hereafter. If you don't, there will be everlasting punishment. Hence in the past, religions and governments went hand in hand and needed each other and supported each other. Both need people to obey laws and it has to be said for all its mistakes and cruelties that religion has helped in civilizing mankind. It has also been and continues to be one of the greatest sources of human misery, harshness and death. Prelates of the past, and even the present in the case of Islam, dish out death sentences to people whom they judge to be guilty without batting an eyelid. In fact, it is usually done in the warm glow of self-righteousness that comes from being 'in touch' with god. The greatest massacres ever committed involving innocent civilians [short of those by Hitler and Stalin] have been carried out in the name of one religion or another and these even targeted their co-religionists. History is littered with the tales of massacres of Christian on Christian, Muslim on Muslim, Christian on Muslim, and vice versa. This was usually with the full knowledge and often the blessing of the highest ecclesiastical and/or civil authorities. This can lead to what normal people would consider a touch of hypocrisy. Sometimes these higher authorities would know one another and even get on but still send their soldiers to fight each other. A prime example of this was Richard 1st of England and the Sultan Saladin. These two met and got on well with each other but still killed thousands of each others' soldiers including the massacre of prisoners. It might be as well to point out that in the Christian church the 6th commandment says 'Thou shalt not kill', full stop. There are no ifs or buts of any kind yet the church has over the centuries killed millions and not only that but gone out of its way to do so in the vilest manner. Torture, hanging, drowning and burning are but a few examples of the methods used by the church to despatch supposed miscreants.

Religious leadership imparts power, not only religious but often temporal as well. In Christianity the Papacy is a classic example. For 1500 years Popes gathered about themselves tracts of land usually left to the church by the wealthy in the hope that it would ease their way to heaven. They ruled not only the church but these lands as well and, as the years went by, these became mini-states and the Popes became kings like any other and did all the things, both good and bad, that temporal rulers of the same period did. It is difficult to read of the lives of many of the Popes during that period and accept that they really believed in a life hereafter. If they really believed in an all-seeing, all-knowing God and the concept of heaven and hell then they would not have committed the many heinous crimes that they did. Crimes such as murder or even plotting it, would most certainly have earned them a spell in hell and you feel this ought to have tempered their actions. These were supposedly men of god, in fact god's supreme representatives on earth. Hence the simple conclusion you have to draw is that they did not really believe. The Popes are, of course, privy to a great deal of secret knowledge which they will not release into the public domain. Over the years there have been many stories of book and parchment finds which have quickly found their way into the hands of the Vatican and thereafter into oblivion as far the general public is concerned. This has inevitably led to speculation that in actual fact the Vatican has incontrovertible evidence that Christ was just an extraordinary man and not the son of God. However, there are plenty who would maintain that even if this were so it would not negate the religion itself, and that it would still have validity.

Islam is not immune from similar accusations. As recently as the Ayatollah Khomeni's return to Iran in February 1979 and his assumption of authority, do we see mass killings for the sake of power, albeit dressed in a religious gown. Khomeni came to power on the back of the human rights excesses of the temporal ruler, the Shah. Khomeni ruled over a supposedly religious regime made up almost exclusively of mullahs, which was instrumental in the death by execution of more people than the Shah was ever accused of. These religious executions are still happening today, with Iran second only to China in the number of people it executes per annum. The deaths, often carried out by the cleric judges themselves, are usually in public and gather great crowds. The condemned are usually hanged by winching the rope up by crane and watching the victim slowly strangled to death. All very humane! The difference is that the Shah did it in the name of temporal power and was overthrown, whilst Khomeni did it in the name of god and seems to have become the Islamic equivalent of a saint. The only slight excuse for Khomeni is that the Koran, unlike all other scriptures of the major religions, does demand the death penalty for a fair number of sins. These include a few that most civilized people would call trivial, such as adultery, apostasy and blasphemy and also in Iran and Saudi Arabia particularly, that of having sex out of wedlock. Imagine that law being introduced in Europe; there would not be many girls left. It is not, of course, a joking matter, because sharia law can be cruel in the eyes of the West. There are two documentary films that ought to be compulsory viewing in every school in the country for the over 16s [because they are too traumatic to be shown to younger pupils], namely 'Death of a Princess' and 'The execution of a teenage girl'. In the latter a 16-year-old Iranian girl was raped several times by a family man and then she was accused of adultery and sentenced to death. She was hanged by the judge himself on the end of a crane jib in public as an example to other girls whilst the accused man, who was not punished at all, actually looked on. Both of these documentaries were made by the BBC and amply illustrate the workings of sharia law in its full barbarity. Young Muslims, living in the comfort and safety of European laws, have no understanding of how harsh and even brutal sharia law can be. The showing of these films would add greatly to their education.

What religions do in general is lay down rules for social living. Society needs rules and religion provides one set. These are backed up by the promise of reward or punishment in the hereafter. God, who sees all and knows all and is somehow omnipresent, will be the judge and jury when you appear before him. However, on the basis that this has never worked very well and human beings continually find excuses to sin, the church (particularly in bygone times) and the mosque (even today) have their own courts and sentence people to some pretty horrible earthly punishments as back-up to God. This in itself seems a touch illogical if not downright unfair. If God is so all-pervasive and the ultimate dispenser of true justice it seems a bit unjust to get disciplined on earth, too, or perhaps he takes this into account with a bit of remission? You really have to wonder why He needs so much help from his earthly representatives. It would of course, have nothing to do with sustaining the personal power of priest, monk or mullah.....

One of the main reasons for the gradual demise of Christianity in Europe is the fact that it can no longer back up its threat of eternal damnation. Over the last century the Church has lost the power it once had to meet out earthly punishment. It has, therefore, to rely purely on faith and the belief of the populace in eternal life. Here we have a slight dichotomy. The Church preaches forgiveness – ask for it and it shall be given. In simplistic terms Christ died so that we may be forgiven [this in itself is a bit hard to equate with any form of justice, and proves that if there is a God and he was Christ's father then apparently he was not too bothered about his suffering. If he is so all-pervasive surely he could have found a much better way?]. Therefore it does not matter how bad we are as long as we ask for, and are genuine in, a request for repentance. Yet we are assured that everyone has to go through a period of purgatory. This seems to be a halfway house between heaven and hell but includes some suffering. So here we discover, prescribed by the basic tenets of an all-forgiving church, that actually we do not receive complete forgiveness and no matter how good you are on earth the route to paradise is somewhat thorny. This, to an increasingly well-educated and justice- minded public, is quite a difficult concept to sell, or accept. Most priests asked to justify the conundrum will present a variety of old and hackneyed phrases such as, 'God moves in a mysterious way'. Or they will delve into the depths of philosophy in an attempt at obfuscation. These explanations really no longer hold water.

The power of any religion rests in its ability to act as a conduit between earth and the hereafter. It has to serve as a mouthpiece for the hereafter which we are told in heaven's case is a place of the purest beauty and tranquillity etc., or better known as paradise, and therefore totally desirable and where we all want to be. In the case of hell it is everything that you fear most and find most loathsome all wrapped up in one along with a fire that burns but never kills. But, and this is a big BUT, no one in the entire history of mankind has glimpsed, or had any proof, or even any communication that we can call rational, with anything heavenly or hellish, or from anyone who has been there and come back to tell the tale . There are plenty who profess to have heard, witnessed, felt or seen things godly [but seldom ungodly, funnily enough, except in the case of exorcism which seems to be the church's way of dealing with mental problems] and they often persuade people to believe them. History is littered with people who have seen visions or heard words directly from God or one of the many saints or angels, or perhaps more often than most, the Virgin Mary. No cases have ever been provable and often there has been an ulterior motive. A close look at their religious credentials usually proves a bit threadbare. Both God and his opposite number [the Devil, Beelzebub, Lucifer, Satan, or whatever you want to call him] are unprovable, unseeable and absolutely unseen, untouchable and in reality, cannot possibly exist. However, in people's minds they do exist and this is mainly because many need a symbol to prove the opposite and, as part of education, to scare the young into believing and therefore behaving. It is the desire of most people to be immortal that perpetuates their existence. If you believe there is nothing when you die the gods

12

cease to exist. However, it is fair to say that even for people who don't believe, that wish can still remain and it is nigh impossible to extinguish. It is easier in general to believe, or perhaps 'hope' is a better word, that there is life after death. It is far more comforting and perhaps some consolation for the trials and tribulations of life on earth. It is also safe to say that if there is no God most people would wonder why mankind exists. This is, of course, an ever-present and most perplexing question unless you believe that the universe did just happen at the start of the Big Bang. In which case there is no other reason for the presence of mankind or everything else, except that we do just happen to be. However, many people who do not believe in God, when asked about the hereafter, will still express a hope in it, often in the vaguest possible terms, but nonetheless they can't really believe that their time on earth is their only time.

The death of a father, mother, child, partner or any close relative or friend is always a traumatic experience. Its inevitability is something that we often find difficult to accept and when we are young life does seem to go on for ever and death is not in the equation. However, when it is, how do people cope? The answer is, of course, by turning to religion. This gives us the assurance that the dearly departed one has gone to a better place and in time will be met again. The epitaph put on my own mother's grave by my father is very apt; it reads '*I cannot think this is goodbye*'. This helps soothe the pain of loss and, of course, in the absence of any other consolation, then religion is there to help and reassure. The easiest way to relieve the pain is to promise that you will meet again, although not explained is how the meeting would go if you really disliked the deceased.

Death also highlights the many anomalies in religion, particularly Christianity. What the Church does is to assure the bereaved that their loved one has gone to a better place and will be in eternal rest and peace. This is standard at funerals, the preacher will beseech God to accept the deceased's soul into heaven and then assure the bereaved that this has happened. In our distress we would like to believe but often, along with this, we know full well that the deceased was one of the biggest sinners, certainly in the eyes of the Church. But the preacher has never met him or her and cannot possibly know what they were like in life. So we conveniently forget purgatory or hell, to one of which is exactly where [if we are to believe the Church's teachings in full] the departed's soul must go. In reality, if there is such a place as hell, that's where he or she is more likely to be headed, but a pastor at a funeral would never dream of mentioning that.

Another problem with an all-powerful, all-seeing, compassionate God is to explain why should He create such grave problems for mankind in general. Religions tie themselves in knots trying to explain this one away. Man 'creates his own problems', and 'free will', are amongst the commonest answers. This, however, is not the case as we all know, and can plainly see when we look around us. A compassionate, forgiving God, the one we are all told about, creates diseases with which we cannot cope, natural disasters like earthquakes and volcanic eruptions which we will never be able to control, together with storms and waves that wipe out whole communities. Throughout the world, when these tragedies happen it is always the innocent, i.e. children, old people, [although they may not be so innocent,] and animals, that suffer most and they are totally incapable of helping themselves. Why would a benevolent god create cancer, bubonic plague, cholera - to mention but a few of the nasties that surround us - and always attack the most vulnerable? If there is a God who created all these tribulations as part of His grand scheme of things then he must be seen as quite a malevolent being, or have a sick sense of humour. Giving man free will may well explain the horrors that we visit upon ourselves but not the suffering of innocents from what we euphemistically call, 'Acts of God'. The death of a million babies a year in Africa alone cannot ever be explained by religion in logical terms that the average person can understand, and no matter how hard we try it never seems to make any real sense. Islam is perhaps one faith with the most simplistic answer. It would just point out that it is 'God's will', an answer that is given for any unanswerable question. But here again why should God wish ill upon his subjects unless he is a malicious being?

Great disasters such as earthquakes and tsunamis are regularly seen as God's punishment on a sinful people. The total illogicality of such a sentiment ensures it comes from people incapable of seeing the wider picture. The Pakistan/Kashmir earthquake of 2005 killed about 80,000 people. Days after it happened there were people interviewed on film blaming some poor women in the hills for dressing immodestly. So God kills 80,000 of the poorest, most wretched people on earth because some women did not cover their heads properly! It really beggars belief that people can think that way except through lack of education. Religion, where it is the only form of education, teaches that God is omnipotent and mere mortals should not question but just accept whatever is thrown at them. The earthquake struck in the mountains of north east Pakistan. This is an incredibly remote area, served by hardly any roads and with no electricity or running water. Schools, shops and other amenities are few and far between. The inhabitants eke out a sparse living from barren mountainsides. Just about the only thing the people have going for them is religion which at least promises something better in the afterlife. They are naturally devout, unlike, for example, those living in the fleshpots of Islamabad, a city actually on the doorstep of the earthquake region. Here, in the eyes of the mosque, all manner of sin and corruption resides and yet God, in his wisdom, picks the poor and hungry living in the mountains. Here He is Allah the God of Islam who is, in actual fact the same as the God of the Christians and the Jews although a visiting alien may be forgiven for doing a bit of head scratching. We then fly across the world to Central America where in Nicaragua in October of the same year we have the Christian God visiting his most ardent supporters with a hurricane of vast magnitude causing landslides which engulf whole villages to such a depth that it is not even worth trying to dig out the dead and, instead the whole village is declared a mass grave. Thousands of the poorest and most devout Christians are killed whilst the fleshpots of the capital Managua are untouched. The scenario is the same. Never mind the really sinful, but instead target the weakest, poorest people for whom life is a constant struggle and who probably pray everyday for a little help from God in order to alleviate their miserable lives. So the good Christian God sends a mud slide to add to their problems and it is called 'an act of God'. The same can be said for China. There, a river floods and wipes out thousands of poor peasants and the Confucian or Taoist god or perhaps even the communist god, [none of which really are gods but philosophies] are called upon for help but the result is always the same, i.e. it is the poorest and the most vulnerable people in society who suffer most. If there is only one God and every religion claims this except for the likes of Chinese religions which actually have a 'path to follow' rather than a supreme being to obey, they cannot all be right and it certainly can be argued that God is not the nice compassionate being in whom we are all led to believe. In fact, if there really is a 'God the Creator' then you feel that the whole universe would be a lot simpler for it seems inconceivable that even a God could create such a complicated conglomeration as earth, the planets, the universe and all that goes with it from the tiniest microbes to the biggest star. Furthermore, perhaps is He still at it, for according to the top scientists the outer cosmos is still expanding?

that it only became apparent to the communist government in Moscow and they were not about to publicise it. Because of the strict secrecy within the communist state the plight of these poor people was not realised in the West until decades later and all the while well-meaning left-wing politicians in the West were praising Stalin for his brilliant policies. It should also be pointed out that those suffering were devout Orthodox Christians, who prayed fervently for some sort of relief or deliverance from the tribulations which were all instigated by their own government, but none came, and a slow death by starvation was their lot. Somehow God had forgotten them or perhaps their prayers were not loud enough which is just as well because Stalin would have had them shot for praying. But if ever there was a case for God's intervention then it was there. The communist state was atheist, was destroying churches, was persecuting all religions and was visiting famine on its own devoutly Christian people. In total ignorance no one came to their aid and nary a word was ever said in their support from the West.

Ethiopia in the 70s was hit by a severe drought and the government was incapable of doing anything for the masses who were starving. These too were devout Coptic Christians and prayers went up all over the land and particularly in the churches. The holy men were incapable of helping apart from prayers – the Coptic Church is a particularly poor one amongst the Christian churches of the world, if not the poorest. Nothing happened until the journalist Michael Burk heard of the plight and went to see for himself. His film so shocked the world, especially the West, that aid poured in and people gave freely to help, although thousands had already died and as usual most were children, thousands were saved by this intervention. This happens time and time again and it matters not which religion is involved, for the weak, the innocent, the aged and those who cannot fend for themselves are the ones who suffer. The rich, or even moderately well off, always find a way to survive and can manage. There must be a moral in this tale somewhere......

RANT 2: ON ISLAM

Islam is the West's next *bête noire*. In fact it has been that for a long time but, in general, has been able either to live with it or ignore it. Times have changed. There are certain branches of Islam flexing their muscles once again. It has happened once before when the Arabs invaded pagan North Africa and carried on into Christian Spain. Not content with this they then turned their attentions to the east, sweeping across the plains of Persia through Afghanistan and on into India. Then after a rest of a few centuries they went on, in the form of the Islamic Ottoman Turks, to conquer the Eastern Roman Empire creating a vast empire and forcibly converting most of its subjects. Today, however, these militant, fundamentalist branches of Islam have modern and very dangerous technology on their side. They also have big ideas of converting the world to their brand of Islam and imposing the rule of sharia law. To achieve their ends they appear willing to use any means, no matter how brutal. They have been, in recent times, responsible for some of the most horrendous atrocities around the world. The suicide bomber appears to be the favoured method and seems to be ever present throughout the world. It is also evident that it is of no consequence to them whom they kill, be they Christian, Hindu, or for that matter Muslim. It is the way of western life that they particularly dislike and if their co-religionists want to live with the infidels then they must accept the consequences. There are, of course, always apologists who are prepared to excuse these excesses and give, in their eyes, competent reasons why they happen. In truth the real reason is that they are fanatic fundamentalists and if taken at its word, Islam, in comparison to most other religions, has a very harsh side to it. Whilst the Koran is full of compassion and charity, when it comes to misdemeanours many of its prescribed punishments are fairly brutal. The fanatics see the Koran as a blueprint for the way that life

21

should be led, even if this is not actually what the majority who follow the religion want. Islam is also quite ruthless when it feels threatened, and with the gradual westernisation of societies in general, it is threatened.

The religion was created in the barren deserts of Arabia by a warrior who saw all around him chaos, idolatry, and continual tribal and family feuding. He wanted to bring order and peace mainly to enhance trade and hence wealth. Mohammed studied the monotheistic religions of the Jews and Christians in Jerusalem. He admired the order these seemed to bring to society in comparison to the multi-theistic idol worship that existed on the Arabian peninsular. The idea of an unseen god, and the hold it appeared to have on its followers, seemed much better for an ordered society. An invisible god is impossible to prove or disprove. In very simplistic terms, he set about dissimulating his ideas which were, it is fair to say, very similar both to Judaism and Christianity. What he did was to adapt the same philosophy to the culture of the Arabian peninsular. He even used the same god. He introduced most of the Old Testament forefathers into his religion and even accepted Christ as a prophet. He just made sure that, in his version, he was the last and final prophet so there could be no more after him and no true religion could be based on the teachings of any prophet before him. He was very unpopular when he started, so much so, that he was once drummed out of Mecca, when the locals saw him as a threat to their way of life. However, this was not a man to be resisted once he had an idea. He gathered a band of followers which grew with time. When it became big enough he turned it into a well-organised army and with the help of the sword he began the process of imposing his ideas initially on the people of Medina, Mecca and Jeddah, and then the rest of the Arabian peninsular. The slash of the sword was accompanied by holy words that came to him directly from his unseen god. These 'talks with God' leant credence to his success in the field, which was extraordinary, and as success breeds success, so his following grew rapidly. This, in turn, gave him the power and the confidence to continue the expansion. Having defeated and unified a large part of the Arabian peninsular he decided he needed back-up. Here he did a very Christ-like thing, disappearing for 40 days into the desert and when he returned he proposed a set of rules that were, in his words, 'not man-made but came directly from God', and therefore could never be changed. Man-made laws can be changed or even just ignored should the people not like them. But here was a set of laws directly from 'God' that dictated how society should live, along with the rewards and punishments. The rewards were, of course, mainly of the heavenly type. They were almost a direct copy of the Jewish and Christian models but the punishments were earthly and administered by the holy men. These rules were added to from his words, written down and they became the Koran. Unlike the bible which leaves judgement and punishment to God, following death, the Koran specifies sins and the method of their punishment here on earth. Many of these are, by Western standards, extremely harsh. However, because they are written in sharia law they cannot be changed. It should, of course, be remembered that the environment in which they were conceived was comfortless, the people fiercely independent and fairly violent, and they were fashioned to match this situation, and they did. In the context of the time and setting in which they were written, they were probably quite reasonable. However, unlike the bible, which has been modified with the passing of time, the Koran has not and, to Muslims, cannot be. It contains many laws that to western civilization are unacceptable. Islam calls itself a compassionate religion and the Koran is full of caring and compassionate advice and yet it prescribes the death penalty for quite a number of misdemeanours. It is not just that it is the death penalty, which is bad enough, but death by the most hideous and painful means imaginable. For example, the penalty for adultery, not seen as a great

23

crime by most people in the west, is death by stoning. The culprits, once sentence has been passed, are taken to a public square on the following Friday, the Islamic equivalent of Sunday when people are not at work and, with stones provided, they literally are stoned to death by the public. This still happens in countries where sharia law is the law of the land. This is a particularly brutal, slow and lingering death and can not be justified by anyone with the slightest ounce of compassion, yet the mullahs making the judgement, are quite happy to support it and hand it out as a sentence without appeal and, on occasions, will be there to assist the execution. And what of the people who throw the stones? You must presume that they enjoy it or they would not go, except, of course, it is the *Will of Allah*. To throw stones at someone until he dies is not the sort of thing that compassionate or civilized people do.

Another of Mohammed's objectives was to keep his flock intact, so the Koran prescribes death for any apostate. However, it is not just death, it is incumbent on the apostate's family to act as executioners and do the killing. Today there are plenty of Muslims, mainly Arabs, living in Europe and the United States in fear of their lives because they have converted to another religion. If a member of their family manages to kill them, this is not considered to be murder in the eyes of sharia law but is seen as justice and, therefore, totally acceptable. Normal murder, of course, carries the death penalty and this is usually by beheading or hanging in a public place on a Friday. These executions are always given advance publicity to attract the maximum number of people to watch. All very compassionate! The only positive argument that can be made for this sort of punishment is that in some countries where sharia law is practised, the crime rate is very low. However, in the case of changing your religion, most Christians would argue that this should all be part of free thought and personal choice. It should be remembered that the Christian church used to kill apostates by burning them but this was stopped

24

about 250 years ago. Sharia law also prescribes mutilation, such as chopping off a hand or a foot, for crimes such as theft and this too is always carried out in public as a deterrent. It is an odd fact that wherever a theocracy is in power, and Iran is a good example, punishment seems to be excessively severe and always in the name of God. It is justified by the argument that the judgement is that of God through his servants on earth, the mullahs. This is also given as the reason for not allowing appeals. If the verdict has come from God then it cannot be wrong, and therefore there is no need to complicate proceedings with appeals. In countries where sharia and statute law are mixed, appeals may be allowed and would be heard by a judge rather than a mullah. However, if the mullahs were to get their way there would be no appeal against a sharia court.

Sharia law is, in fact, what many rulers in the Middle East really like. It is hard but straightforward, and severe if not downright cruel, but with penalties which are accepted totally by a compliant public. This is because they come from the Koran which came directly from the word of God through his prophet Mohammed. This makes these laws unchangeable, ergo, it follows that Islam makes a bad bedfellow of democracy when sharia law is the law of the land. Democracy means, in broad terms, giving power to the people and that, of course, would mean taking it away from the mullahs which would be un-Islamic and therefore a sin. As the excesses of the rulers in Iran get more publicity, so opposition to their rule is growing, but very slowly. However, the religious have a standard answer and it is always to cry foul by pointing out that such opposition is against the word of God. The problem is that the less sophisticated in society, and there are many such in Iran, believe them. The Taliban in Afghanistan, probably one of the most squalid regimes ever to rule in the name of religion, were a classic example of this. Had it not been for their support of terrorism they would probably still be in power today, for they had massive support particularly amongst the old conservative male population. Whilst in command they wielded absolute power absolutely. They held public executions at the drop of a hat and often for offences that even under sharia law did not warrant the death penalty particularly when it applied to women. The word *taliban* actually means 'students', but, as often happens with religious regimes, the people who actually gained power were fairly poorly educated and certainly unsophisticated when it came to wielding power. They still have their supporters, particularly in some of the more remote areas of Afghanistan and North West Pakistan, and also among the more fundamentalist Islamic populations of the Middle and Far East. Judged by the standards of educated Western man, there was nothing 'holy' and nothing particularly compassionate about the Taliban, and the same can be said for the regime of mullahs in Iran. What can be said in their defence is that they really believe, with a passion, that they are following the Koran to the letter and, therefore, are right in every way and no argument will convince them otherwise. This is similar to the Jesuits, whose motto was *'Give me the child until he is seven and I will give you the man'*, and who would use any method, including the rod, to instil in their young wards total submission to God and the Roman Catholic religion. They, too, were utterly convinced that they were doing the right thing. The mullahs of today use similar methods and do instil a total belief in the young. The first task of primary schools in Islamic states is to teach the children to learn the Koran by rote. They sit in their classes for hours on end chanting the verses of the Koran in unison until they know them off by heart. The problem is that the mullahs are unable to stand back and look at the world objectively. They cannot see that the world is changing and that perhaps their religion may also have to change. What is surprising is that even most educated Muslims dare not speak out against these regimes no matter how odious they are. Islam discourages any questioning of its doctrines. Islamic religious men are very single- dimensional. It is Islam or nothing, which makes most debate with Christian leaders somewhat pointless. The Christians enter such talks in good faith and are prepared to bend over backwards to try and accommodate their Islamic 'brothers', but for Islam it is impossible to acknowledge that any another religion could conceivably be right, let alone co-exist. British-born and -bred Muslims who become radicalised fundamentalists believe in the conversion of the whole population of the country. Their argument is that Islam is the only religion and that sharia law is the only valid law and so everybody should be made to follow it. This view brooks no discussion amongst fundamentalists, and so it is impossible to have a constructive argument. The more progressive and sophisticated Islamic states, such as Egypt and Turkey, do try to keep religion out of politics but it is an uphill struggle. The governing classes in these countries are terrified that an Islamic fundamentalist party will be elected every time there is a vote. Turkey is a good example of this, for they do have genuine elections involving a plethora of political parties. These include fundamentalist Islamic parties and it takes the army to safeguard the constitution. This insists that Turkey must remain a secular state, and in the past when this status has been jeopardised, even in a democratic election, the army has threatened a military coup. In Algeria it actually happened. A fundamentalist party was voted into power and the army staged a coup which led to a bloody civil war in which the fundamentalists seemed to rejoice in going into small outlying villages in the dead of night and cutting as many throats as possible, including those of women and children. They still managed, somehow, to justify this on religious grounds although the murdered people all were Muslims.

In less sophisticated countries such as Saudi Arabia the royal family keeps power by means of a good secret service, a rabid religious police force, but especially by posing as the keepers of the holy places [Mecca and Medina] and by allowing the religious police total freedom to do as they wish. These zealots roam the streets wielding long canes and beat anyone who is a bit tardy entering the mosque after the muezzin has called the faithful to prayer. Refusing to go would earn not only a good beating but instant imprisonment. This would be called fairly uncivilized behaviour in the West, if not assault. However, it is part of their culture and accepted as normal.

The mullahs of Islam are often fairly unsophisticated with little higher education apart from reading and learning the Koran. Knowledge of the Koran is the main criterion for becoming a holy man, because the Koran is seen as a complete model for how to live. This includes politics, and to the average Muslim in the Middle East, religion, the law and politics are inseparable. These people, in general, are not great carers or counsellors of people unless the question is on a point of religion. All they really want is for the law to be obeyed as laid down in the Koran, no matter whom it hurts. The schools or madrassas in the more remote areas of the Middle and Far East only teach children how to read and rote-learn the Koran, the rest of their education is fairly elementary. In general, Islam says there can only be one interpretation of the Koran but like all religions there are differing opinions which has led to different sects such as the Sunnis, Shiites and one of the most militant, the Wahabis of Saudi Arabia, amongst others. Like Christians of old, they do not really like each other and regard one another as heretics. Although they normally live together in peace, it can easily, and often does, lead to conflict when they will kill each other with impunity. Letting off bombs in public places has, somehow, become quite acceptable provided that the cause is right. A good example of this was the praise heaped upon the 9/11 suicide bombers by Osama bin Laden [head of al-Qa'eda]. Bin Laden is seen as a holy man by many Muslims and they call him *sheikh* which has religious connotations. The fact that he personally planned the murder of some 3000 people in the most hideous fashion, among whom were many of his co-religionists, does not seem to bother them. In actual fact, Islam has a long and well documented history of suicide killers. The word assassin comes directly from an Islamic sect called the Hashshashin. The founder and leader of this sect was one Rashid ed-Din Sinan. He was an Iraqi Shiite who lived in the mountains of Syria and was known to crusaders as The Old Man of the Mountains. He allowed his followers to smoke hash and whilst under the influence would explain to them what paradise was like. He told them that if they followed his orders to the letter they would gain their place in a wonderful oasis peopled with beautiful women, for that is how he described it. He let it be known to all and sundry that he was for hire should anyone wish to be rid of an enemy. The victim was invariably someone's political opponent. Often non-believers such as Christians were not only the victims but also were involved in hiring his services. However, he was certainly not averse to killing Muslims. Assassination was his *metier* and if the money was right, his followers killed to order. He certainly entertained some top crusaders and Muslims, and did their bidding. Because the perpetrators had to get close enough to stab their victim they very seldom got away, so it was assumed by all concerned that it was a suicide mission. This, of course, has strong echoes today. Organisations like Hammas usually are run by venerable old mullahs who spend their time preaching murder. They tell their young followers that their place in paradise will be assured because what they are about to do is in the name of Islam and they will be considered martyrs. These young and gullible people are brainwashed into believing that what they are doing is the will of Allah. Suicide is forbidden in Islam but the mullahs seem to get around this by arguing that they are soldiers dying in a 'holy war'. However, how a cleric can order a person to go into a bar or restaurant full of innocent people, blow them up and then justify the act as war, is beyond comprehension. The most notable thing about these clerics is that they are never the ones who go out with bombs strapped to their waists; instead it is always the young and impressionable foot soldiers. The picture of martyrdom and Islamic paradise that is offered to young men, where they can have their pick of young, exceptionally beautiful virgins, may be an enticing one, but we have yet to hear what is offered to the young women who sacrifice themselves.

There is a great problem with any religion that is set in stone. The world evolves, times and people change, and civilization supposedly gets more mature and thoughtful, although this is questionable, too. However, with Islam, you have an unchangeable set of rules, jealously guarded by a large proportion of fairly unsophisticated clergy with an immense hold over a relatively poorly educated flock. Alongside this, is the fact that should anyone suggest a change it would be seen as a heresy by a large section of the mullahs and no doubt prompting a *fatwa* [a declaration condemning someone to death] to be proclaimed on the life of the miscreant. This does not make it easy to speak out against anything that appears in the Koran. Freedom of thought let alone speech, when it comes to the Koran, is an absolute no-no. Islam brooks no criticism whatsoever and recently there have been outbursts of rage across the Islamic world at a group of cartoons supposedly depicting Mohammed. There were calls for the death, by beheading, of the journalists who dared to draw and publish such images. These were seen as immense provocations by the Islamic world and the Danish government was quick to apologise and even grovel. However, you never hear even the slightest protest from any western government, all of whom are nominally Christian, when Christians are murdered in Iraq, Iran and Pakistan simply because they are Christians. Churches are regularly desecrated and often even burned to the ground. This is acceptable behaviour to Muslims because they do not believe other religions should exist. This happens several times every year and it does not even make a couple of lines in the western press. This can justifiably be called provocation but Christians dare not retaliate for fear of further reprisals. However, if it were the other way round and Muslims were killed by Christians, the whole of Islam would be up in arms. It never ceases to amaze how easily the Islamic world can be offended for what it sees as the slightest insult or provocation. Yet Muslims feel they can insult, provoke, and even kill people of other religions without a murmur. The stone Buddhas, carved from the rock on the side of a mountain in Afghanistan, and which were destroyed by the Taliban, are a good example. Whilst the world protested, mildly, at this barbarity Muslims kept silent. After the cartoons incident the world got used to pictures of sweet, innocent-looking Islamic girls, heads dutifully wrapped in headscarves, parading down London streets, carrying banners demanding beheadings. This was not an edifying sight and actually, they should have been prosecuted, for they were breaking the law, but as usual no action was taken. Had it been a Christian demonstration, anyone holding a banner seeking the death of a Muslim would undoubtedly been arrested and charged by our brave boys in blue.

Another problem is that there are second- and third-generation Muslims in the West who tend to support their co-religionists in far-off countries over their allegiance to their country of birth. Their religion seems to take precedence over their national allegiance. This is not a problem that Britain has experienced with immigrants in the past. They have tended to become British within a generation. Witness the demonstrations in the UK against the war in Iraq, and the fight in Afghanistan, because these are universally unpopular and are challenged by as many, if not more, British Christians than Muslims. Yet the 7/7 bombings were the ultimate example of Muslims feeling that they have to do something to teach the Christians a lesson. Contrast this with the constant harassment that Christians have to put up with all over the Middle East simply because Muslims assume that they support the West, which in general is untrue. Churches are regularly burned to the ground and

31

men, women and children are hounded out of their homes, and often killed, because their allegiance is in doubt although without a scrap of evidence. Prior to the war in Iraq, there were about one million Arab Christians living in Iraq. Since the invasion many have been killed, most of their churches destroyed, and well over 400,000 have fled the country. These were Iraqi Christians whose loyalty to their country was never in question.

Whenever a mullah speaks, he does so in the name of Allah and everyone better believe him for woe betide those who do not. Even the well educated have to watch what they say. To venture an opinion that the Koran or its spokesmen might be wrong is to court disaster for this can instantly be labelled as blasphemy and any form of blasphemy is punishable by death. At the dawn of Islam and before the mullahs became all-powerful, the Arab nation was streets ahead of the rest of the world, except perhaps for China, in their scientific and mathematical knowledge as well as their literature and art and, in fact, all forms of learning. Their scholars, who were plentiful at the time, had carefully collected both Greek and Roman texts, learned from them, and were taking that learning on to further heights. At the same time the Roman Catholic Church, with the papacy at it head, was all-powerful in Europe, and doing its level best to spike any advances in learning. Even the average monk was not very well educated but the church jealously guarded knowledge for itself. It only took one relatively uneducated monk to cry blasphemy to put a scholar under investigation and he was then in serious trouble and lucky to get away with his life. Gradually over the centuries the roles changed. As the power of the church diminished, learning, and specifically scientific learning, increased, ironically, a lot of it coming from the Arab world and often via the crusaders. At the same time the power of the mosque was growing and Arab scholars were being reined in, and learning in the Islamic world, was being curtailed. The mosque believes that all the learning

terrorist is totally committed to losing his or her life on the basis that it is Allah's will, then prevention is almost impossible. Hence, the success of the 9/11 gang, the 7/7 London bombers, and the continuing insurgency in Iraq. The big question is how can so many people be persuaded willingly to give up their lives in the cause of Islam? The simple answer is, through total devotion and belief in their religion. They can be likened to the Christian martyrs of bygone eras who believed that they were right and were prepared to die for their beliefs in the sure knowledge that they would go to heaven. The sad thing is that we do not hear a united voice from Islamic clerics condemning suicide terrorism for the abomination it is. If they were to preach the message that this behaviour was, actually, a deadly sin, and according to some mullahs it is, things could be different. If the perpetration of such an act would condemn the perpetrator to eternal hell and damnation instead of paradise, it might sew a seed of doubt in his mind. This, perhaps, could dissuade him from committing the act in the first place. Until this happens, and as long as fundamentalist Muslims stay as devout as they are, and mullahs preach that it is martyrdom not suicide, it is very difficult to see how this sort of terrorism can effectively be stopped. However, the chances of the last point happening are nil. First, there is no single head of any of the Islamic sects such as exists, for example, in the Christian church. Furthermore, like all religions, Islam does have its splits, even though it likes to think otherwise. Add to this the fact that many Islamic clerics actually believe in the destruction of all other religions by any means. Just like the Roman Catholic church of old, if a few of their own get killed in the process it does not really matter for 'God will know and look after his own'. Furthermore there is the point that violence is an integral part of Islam and not only in the context of punishment. When Mohammed demanded that Islamic soldiers go out and convert the infidels, he proposed that the use of the sword would

34

help. Effectively, this sanctioned conversion to Islam using the threat of violence or death.

The burning question today is can the West and Islam co-exist? Fundamentally, the answer is probably 'yes' but while fundamentalists on both sides continue to proliferate, it will be an uneasy co-habitation. In Europe, as religious fervour recedes, people find it difficult to understand how profoundly are held the beliefs that Muslims have for their religion. In fact 'deep belief' in the West is really a thing of the past. Fundamentalist Christians have similar entrenched beliefs but they are now a minority in Europe and they are mainly concentrated in the United States. However, they do feel deeply about religion and they tend to feel the same way about Islam as Islam does about them. Nevertheless, the higher echelons of the Christian church are prepared to talk, or at least to try and co-exist with Islam. In contrast, if Islam is followed, as it ought to be, via sharia law and the Koran, it cannot really co-exist with any other religions and would have totally to condemn secularism and any form of non-belief. Hence, fundamentalist Islam is inherently anti-democracy and definitely is uncomfortable towards secular western civilization as it exists today. Some moderate mullahs talk to clerics of other religions and will act in unison with them, but in general these inter-faith talks are despised by most of the top mullahs of Iran, Saudi Arabia, and Pakistan. They do not believe in talks with any other religions because there can be no compromise, so therefore, talks are pointless. When the likes of the Mayor of London invites radical Islamic clerics into his office for talks, he displays a certain naivety, for whatever they say, they need not be held to their word for their religion advises that any promise to a non-Muslim can be rescinded without a sin being committed.

It may well be argued that the terrorists are winning. Slowly but surely there are more and more restrictions of freedom being forced upon the populations of the West because of the threat of Islamic terrorism. Ports of entry and departure from countries are becoming increasingly hard to pass through. Security checks are getting burdensome, and the prospect of identity cards and biometric passports is coming ever closer. Freedoms taken for granted 20 years ago are rapidly disappearing. All the politicians do in the face of any protest is hold up their hands and declare that all the measures enacted are for the good and safety of the public. In actual fact, they welcome the situation, for it means that they can keep a tighter grip on the movements and actions of the general public. This is what governments, in general, really want. Too much freedom for the public is seen as a dangerous thing by politicians, and they will go to any lengths to try and curb this, always, of course, with the decision dressed up as being 'for the public good'. Here, we have Islam providing them with a helping hand and despite all the downcast faces and political hand-wringing, there is, actually, some satisfaction that these restrictive measures can be introduced so easily. The sad thing is that, given a poll, many people would probably support the restrictions because the political spin would point only to a short term necessity. Undoubtedly, the dangers for the future that this continual sapping of our freedoms will bring would not be recognised.

In conclusion, it is to be hoped that the, in may ways, great religion of Islam can adapt increasingly to the West. Ideally, it would help its peoples lead more rounded lives whilst preserving the more humane and time honoured values that it represents. Could that become Allah's will?

RANT 3: ON GOVERNMENT, LOCAL AND NATIONAL

From the very beginnings of history and the forming of social groupings among humans, leaders have emerged. Throughout the animal kingdom this usually goes to the strongest and so we can assume it was with early human society. It fell upon this leader to lead and that included keeping some form of order amongst his grouping. When the strongest grew old and weak he was replaced by a younger man who was usually the strongest and he did it by any means possible. This was sanctioned by the group who instinctively wanted order and were prepared to support whoever could offer it – the strongest. Hence we can see that human society needs to be led and has been from the very beginning and this has never changed. What has changed over the years is the way in which we are led. In the past a strong man, and very occasionally a woman, would emerge and he would make the decisions for the group around him. He would also keep order and be judge, jury and executioner if need be, but always backed up by the group. As these groupings became larger and societies began to form, the leader recruited helpers, followers, attendants, or in reality people that would do his bidding. Although this is perhaps a bit of a simplification, it is this grouping that developed into government. Over the ages and by many different paths the power of the leader has diminished and the power of the people has grown into what we in the West call democracy. With all its faults and they are legion, we see this form of government as the best. It certainly gives the populace some powers and conversely diminishes those of the leaders because, every so often, they can be voted out of office. However, even in democracies 'the people' actually have very little power over the broad policy of a government, and in general, governments do as they wish and not necessarily as the electorate wishes. In Britain the government will argue that it has been elected to govern and once in power does not need to go back to the electorate for its opinion no matter how contentious the policy. A good recent example of this was the decision to invade Iraq. Had this been put to a referendum, for example, it is highly unlikely it would have won a majority. But on the basis that our government does not rule by referendum it did not have to ask for permission. On the other hand, in Switzerland they do govern by referenda and all big decisions are put to the people. This does slow down major decision-making but perhaps that is not a bad thing. It gives everyone time to reflect. Plus it must be said that Switzerland is and always has been one of the most successful, most peaceful and most prosperous states in Europe.

Prior to the arrival of democracy, communities, be they small or large, were ruled by kings, queens, despots, dictators, usurpers, religious men, pretenders and even bandits. These rulers were seldom benevolent to the people over whom they ruled. They were in general wealth-seeking nepotists. They kept power to themselves and were jealous of it. They were often portrayed as strong, glorious, weak, good, bad and a few other adjectives but seldom cruel. Yet given the power structures of the time, they were cruel, particularly to the individual. They were beset with the normal problems of ruling, and these included, more often than not, keeping their own power intact and their more over-mighty subjects in order. Seldom were they concerned with the greater good of the people unless the great and mighty were counted as 'the people'. Individuals, particularly those within the lower echelons, did not count except for tax purposes, of course, and this is still true today in our democracy. In ancient times, if the people really did not like their ruler the only way to get rid of him was by rebellion or assassination. Resignation was never an option. Assassination was always by far the easiest and quickest but for this to happen the ruler had to fall out with his nearest and dearest or at least his close friends.

Commoners never got close enough and if they did manage to kill him it meant certain death, for the chances of him getting away were nil. When they decided to do it a new leader was already behind the scenes and just waiting for the call. Rebellion was never the easy option because the ruler usually had an army to back him and no matter how many of his subjects rebelled they were seldom a match for a well-armed and organised army. Such usurpers were always put down in the harshest way with as many deaths as possible during the quelling, and then as many judicial deaths as necessary in the ensuing witch-hunt. All this, of course, was in the name of keeping the peace and as a warning to any other subjects who did not appreciate their leader. Here we are talking about an age long gone, or are we? One of the most chilling statements made by a politician during the second half of the twentieth century was by the much-loved and admired [in his own country, for sure] Ronald Reagan, who while governor of California, spoke on the unrest in university campuses over the war in Vietnam and how to control it. He said, 'if it takes a bloodbath then let's get it over with.' So here we have a top politician who was quite prepared to kill as many 'innocent' students as necessary to stop protests against what was seen by them as an unjust, unnecessary and perhaps illegal war undertaken by the government. It did not do his political prospects any harm whatsoever.

This can and has happened today in what we would call compassionate democracies. If it happens in somewhere like the old South Africa as it did at Sharpeville, all our leaders jump up and down and shake their fists and heap shame on the government and ask what possibly can be expected from such a hard line, right-wing racist government. But they still go on talking to them and what is more relevant – trading with them. However, when it happens on our own hallowed soil as it did on Bloody Sunday in Northern Ireland, when the British army opened fire on British subjects, and from the most creditable accounts, unarmed ones, killing some 13 people and wounding a further 14, this was alright, they were keeping order and it was done in the interests of the majority. The leaders of the day backed the army version of events against the evidence of non-partisan witnesses, including a good mix of journalists. In 1999, 27 years after the event and in the face of two past inquiries both of which could be deemed to have been 'whitewashes', and owing to mounting pressure and disquiet from some parts of the public but mainly from the bereaved, a further inquiry was set up. This has so far cost the taxpayer £163m, is still sitting, and all the bets are that it will come out with another 'whitewash'. This alone proves the total insincerity of governments towards the individual and the fact that you cannot buck the Establishment. They will never admit to doing wrong no matter how the evidence stacks up. In this case we can say that the army opened fire because they were being stoned. People were killed and the force used against the rioters was obviously excessive but as far as the Establishment was concerned it was in line with the need to keep order within society. Our beloved leaders get away with this sort of thing for there is no one better at delay and obfuscation than the Establishment, and although the few, usually the hurt and bereaved, try to keep the pressure up for the truth to come out, the public soon forget and those politicians responsible for the outrage get off scot-free. They are never even censured and usually end up getting a peerage and always handsome pensions. The need for order in society is so great that when it is threatened we tend to rally behind the Establishment and as long as their methods do not impinge on us personally we quickly forgive and/or forget their methods. Had the British government just held up its hands at the time and admitted that a mistake was made, and had apologised, it would today be seen as far more honourable and trustworthy. For sure it would have had to pay compensation to the families of the bereaved but that would have amounted to far less than the lawyers have earned over the years and it would by now have been just another page in the history books. Instead the issue is still in the public domain, the bereaved relatives are still very angry and the government which swears it hates wasting the taxpayer's money carries on shelling out for lawyers in the hope that when the report finally does come out there will not be many of the relatives left alive.

A good current example of this is the American war on terrorism. The British government was quick to support this and has so far agreed with all its methods which include the blanket bombing of areas in Afghanistan. This has inevitably led to many civilian deaths, including women and children, and turning many thousands into refugees. However, few voices are heard in condemnation of these actions. Rather the opposite is true, and many of the operations have actually been applauded by the public and other governments as an essential part of a war which arguably is unwinnable. Other means, perhaps less arbitrary and violent and certainly less conspicuous, were not considered. Afghanistan is an intractable problem and is unsolvable and certainly blanket bombing does not help. The Taliban may have been overthrown but the killing of innocent civilians does nothing for the popularity of an army that is there supposedly to help with reconstruction. The United States had already tried this method in Vietnam where it failed conspicuously. They have not learned very much. It is an odd twist that well-known and used clichés such as 'we learn from history', or 'we learn from our mistakes', actually seldom tend to be true. The two most effective and successful counter- insurgency operations ever were by Britain against the Mau Mau in Kenya, and the communists in Malaya. These campaigns seem now to be completely forgotten but the methods used were very successful, relatively non-violent and could certainly have been used in Afghanistan to far better effect than the insensitive and knuckle-headed approach that was applied.

41

There it has just induced resentment amongst the people and a gradual return of support for the Taliban.

Another example of this was the killing of four students at Kent University, USA in May 1970 by State troopers on the authority of the governor who had banned all demonstrations. The troopers were not facing any threat apart from verbal abuse and the odd stone and bottle. This was a classic example of going totally over the top with force and the result was that four innocent young students were killed and very soon the brouhaha died down and it was all forgotten except, no doubt, by the families. However, in reality the governor should have been prosecuted and a charge of premeditated murder would have been quite in order. In fact, nothing happened, not even a little apology. The sick thing was that the demonstrations had been banned because they were against the federal government sending troops into Cambodia. The even sicker thing was that the four students who were killed were not, in fact, part of the demonstration but innocent passers by. The US is held up, mainly by its own politicians and people, as the land of the free where everyone has constitutional rights and free speech goes without saying. Yet here a local governor banned a peaceful protest march against what many in the country believed was an illegal policy and has since been proven to be so. He got off with not even a rebuke from the higher authorities.

The Tiananmen Square incident in China was a similar case. There was never an armed challenge to the government. A group of students got 'silly' democratic ideas into their heads and held a demonstration demanding to be heard. The government, however, felt threatened and ordered in the military and countless innocent unarmed students were killed. Because of the secrecy of the communist government the true figures will never be known but it is estimated to be in the hundreds. This massacre was one of the most cowardly and despicable acts by any government in the second half of the twentieth century, yet it has done it no lasting harm at home or abroad. Although the rest of the world protested loudly, including of course the United States and the British governments, no one was ever even censured let alone prosecuted nor would this even be considered in a secretive totalitarian state such as China. Not only that, but all the governments in the West after as short a break as possible just resumed normal diplomatic and trading relations. In fact, trading with the West since then has increased to almost overwhelming proportions and Chinese leaders are welcomed and feted in capitals round the world, so their disapproval was clearly not that great. The main difference between these two examples is that the second was perpetrated by a secretive and Draconian communist government whose human rights record is appalling, and the first by a democratically elected one that preaches freedom of speech and human rights to others *ad nauseam*.

Governments are not very caring institutions. The governments of India and Pakistan, both of which countries have vast populations, huge cities and are relatively wealthy, still have and put up with abject poverty, poor or even nonexistent infrastructure, chronic disease and high rates of infant mortality. There are still vast areas where there is no running water, no electricity and where foreign charities keep the local population going with hand-outs of food. Yet these same countries can spend a king's ransom on developing nuclear weapons. It seems utterly obscene that cash that could be spent on ameliorating the harshness of life of the poorest in their countries is diverted to the making of nuclear weapons, and for what reason? To deter each other? India and Pakistan have been to war some five or six times since they achieved independence in 1948 and now that they have these weapons of mass destruction can we expect them to launch these at each other? There is a vague possibility they will, although let's hope that they have more sense. However, the investment would have been far better spent looking

43

after their own citizens, by building hospitals and schools, and introducing running water and electricity. If the governments were genuinely caring that is what they would have done but like most governments they really do not care. Developing nuclear weapons brings them into the nuclear world and this is supposed to give them some sort of national pride. In fact what it does give them, the politicians that is, is personal pride and prestige, and perhaps a bigger say in world affairs, whereas, if there were any justice, it should be 'shame' with a capital S.

So the big question of the day is do we need governments? Unfortunately the answer is an emphatic yes. The very nature of humans and society, no matter how primitive or sophisticated, means that we need governing and without government society quickly breaks down into anarchy. This may suit a very tiny minority but the vast majority within any population will always support order. However, governments do go through swings of power but even the most benign are all-powerful institutions and called upon to act 'in society's interests' [but usually their own], they will. What they call 'society's interests' may differ greatly from what society actually thinks, but once in power a government often feels it can do as it likes. The argument is that once elected on a manifesto it is free to carry it out and act in what it thinks are the 'best interests of the country' as a whole, even if the manifesto promises are ignored. A classic example of swings of power occurred in the late 60s and 70s when a succession of complacent governments allowed the union movement as a whole to become too powerful. This inevitably led to conflict, mainly between employers and the unions, but the latter did get way above themselves and challenged the government's power, too. Governments, both Labour and Conservative, did not know how to deal with this confrontation. They were reluctant to go back to the bad old pre-war days when the military would be called out to use force to put down any confrontation or strike. This

44

usually resulted in the government giving in. The unions became more and more powerful and in the end it was difficult to see who was actually running the country. Whenever there was a major decision on the economy, certainly on the Labour side, the General Secretary of the Trades Union Congress would be called in for talks. Inevitably the economy, which was still struggling to recover from the Second World War and, in actual fact, was still in a fairly parlous state, suffered. Unions controlling the dockers, car workers, steel makers, coal miners and printers held their respective industries to ransom and would strike for the pettiest of reasons. It should be mentioned here that the management was fairly crass, too. But the unions definitely felt that the power was theirs and did as they pleased, including the acceptance of such practices as gross over-manning, turning a blind eye to blatant and massive theft by workers, running closed shops as though they were in the personal gift of the local shop steward, and many other equally ruinous practices. This led directly to the demise of the great ports of London, Liverpool and Hull because ships used to sit around for weeks whilst disputes were sorted out. It also ruined the car industry which just found it impossible to turn out a decent car under such conditions. The press barons who had been based in Fleet Street in London for over 100 years had to abandon the area owing to restrictive practices, and at least one owner even offered his premises free to the unions to run a newspaper themselves but the offer was turned down. The union leaders knew how dishonestly they ran the print floor and could not see themselves running an economic enterprise. Hence it can be said that the unions broke what was left of the old British industry and during that period became far too powerful. The government, as an institution, was never going to put up with this state of affairs and eventually an incoming government would have to reassert its power. As it happened it fell to the formidable Margaret Thatcher. She took them head-on and defeated them. Their power was massively curtailed and apparently with the approval of the majority of people, for unions went from a membership of about 85% of the working population, pre-Thatcher, to less than 45% when membership became voluntary by law. When the Conservatives finally lost power and New Labour took over the unions really believed their powers would be restored but it was not to be, nor will it ever be voluntarily. However, when it suits government it will hold a referendum asking 'the people' for an answer but this happens very seldom and is only done when it is sure the answer it will receive is the one it wants, as was the case in the referendum over entry into Europe.

There is also a constant battle for power between the people at the top of any government or political party. These are perhaps the tensions most hidden from the public and often the least likely to get into the public domain for it is in the antagonist's interest to keep their feuding from view. Throughout Parliamentary history these private feuds have led to good pieces of legislation failing to materialise, [Gladstone in his final years tried to get an Irish Home Rule bill through Parliament and failed mainly because many of the top men in his Liberal party felt is was time for him to go and were vying for the leadership so wanted to defeat him. Had the bill been passed many of the subsequent horrors that occurred with the Irish question may never have happened.]. Other consequences involve able ministers being sacked, [e.g. Heseltine], prime ministers being toppled [e.g. Margaret Thatcher] and countless things being done that should not have been, and vice versa. This all has to do with people in power wanting more of it, and above all else to be top dog which must be the pinnacle of ambition. Hence there is a constant tension between ladder-climbers in even the most harmonious of governments or parties. This often appears when choosing a leader. There have been a number of 'best leaders' that have never made it to the top because of petty or even major jealousies. A couple of classic examples are R. A. Butler who was a very astute man and would probably have made a very good leader but was not chosen by his party. Instead they chose Alec Douglas Home who, to all intents and purposes, was a nonentity and did fail completely as a leader. Michael Heseltine stood for the leadership of the Conservative Party and was beaten by John Major. Heseltine would have made a flamboyant and probably innovative leader but because of internal jealousies he was beaten by 'the grey man' Major who was the very opposite. Here, too, the suggestion can be made that Thatcher did not really want anyone brilliant to follow her as this might have overshadowed her achievements. She therefore, groomed Major for the leadership in the sure knowledge that it would be she who was remembered and not him.

The struggle between the various political parties is always more visible to the general public at times when they are invited to participate with their vote. The shenanigans between the parties seem to bore the public these days judging from the dismal turn out at elections. Nevertheless, the battles are always vocal, often bad tempered, occasionally abusive and sometimes downright malicious. So for the onlookers a general election is always a bit of fun. Take British governments from 1800 through to the present day. In 1800 Parliament was elected by the few, the nobility and the squirearchy. It held power in their interests. Laws that were passed all favoured what they stood for and they were excessively harsh on any of the general populace who broke them, or even dared to question them. There were something like 500 hanging offences on the books. Imprisonment was comfortless and leniency not common. As the century progressed and people power began to grow, a series of reforms was the result. These included a gradual widening of the franchise, [always resented by those who already had the vote], and a lessening in the number of hanging offences, and of sentences for minor offences.

The beginning of the 20th century saw a big rise in the franchise and a further watering down of arbitrary government power. This process continued throughout the first half of the century though interrupted by the two world wars. During these periods the government took fairly stringent powers upon itself in the name of state security. However, in these cases, the national interest came first and most people accepted the situation without murmur. Any that did not were assumed to be enemies of the state and imprisoned although it was careful to call it 'preventative detention'. By the end of the Second World War most people, including some politicians, had had enough of the severe wartime laws. Hence the 50s and 60s were probably the two best decades ever for personal freedoms and a benign *'laissez faire'* state. For example, during the war the state introduced identity cards which had to be carried at all times and produced when demanded for a police officer or other government official of whom there were many. By the early 50s the politicians could see how unpopular they were and they abolished them really in an attempt to curry favour and gain votes. The police, part of the state control system, were the public's friends and our picture of the benign bobby helping an old lady or a kid, really comes from this period. Gradually during the 70s and 80s society became less sociable and caring. Crime started rising, and terrorism crept in, although there had always been an element of this in one form or other for over a century, but it was instigated by nationalist elements in Scotland or Ireland and was a lot less intrusive or destructive. As these problems increased, the government was given the excuse to expand the powers of the police, and of course the police, probably one of the most inefficient arms of government, kept asking for more. The more they received the more crime nevertheless went up, a situation always put down to not enough power and not enough men. All the increases, and they have been considerable since the 60s, do not seem to have done anything for the crime rate but the rights of the man in the street have inexorably

48

the political parties today will not reveal any promises to reduce the power or interference of government. In fact, they all promise to do more to 'help'. This really means taking on more powers and intruding even further into our lives. During the Thatcher years the promise was made that there would be a reduction in local government personnel. By the end of her time in office the numbers had actually increased. No matter what they promise, governments cannot bring themselves to reduce snooping on peoples lives. However, it is a moot point as to whether the great British public could cope any longer with an increase in their personal freedom. Calling it a nanny state is a generous way of putting it, in fact, the more 'nannying' it becomes the more the phrase 'police state' comes to mind.

The leaders we elect and put into power should be upright, honest and generally of good character. They should remember that they are there to serve the people and do their best for the whole community. However, it is sad to say that today many of these standards are no longer met. This is, of course, a huge generalisation but it seems that politicians are in the job for themselves, for their own ego trips, for what they can get out of it financially, and are not necessarily there for the good of the community. Before they are elected they will promise the earth but once in Parliament they are not that good at delivering. A few make quite good constituency MPs but they are in the minority. In general they are elected because they want to become members of what many consider to be the most exclusive club in the world. Few and far between are the cases where individuals have actually been helped by their local MP. If the case is high profile and the MP stands to get a bit of publicity out of it, then he or she may get involved, otherwise there is little chance. Often constituents do not even know what is being done in their name, or supposedly for their sake. The really sad thing is that a reasonable percentage of constituents do not even know who their

MP is. Even worse is the fact that the political establishment today is held in such low esteem that a great many people cannot be bothered to vote and really do not care who represents them. MPs are fully aware of this fact but they do little or nothing to change the situation. It is also a general truism that governments overall do not care for individuals unless, that is, popular support gets behind that individual's case and the government sees some potential kudos for itself in helping. Injustices happen on a daily basis both at home and abroad and it is usually left to the injured parties to sort themselves out. Help from government or local representatives is seldom forthcoming. Those cases that we do hear about tend to be high profile and have the attention of the media. This is the one way of getting aid from those in power. If the media think it is a good story and want to get their teeth into it, then our representatives may decide to move themselves.

Fighting the Establishment is an uphill struggle for an individual. Once the powers that be have made a ruling it is almost impossible to get it reversed. The Establishment does not ever admit to being wrong, no matter how wrong it is subsequently proved to be. Apologies and admissions of incorrect decisions just do not happen these days. Furthermore, politicians, both national and especially in local government never resign and are seldom sacked no matter how big the blunder or the scandal. There have been one or two notable exceptions in the past 25 years but they are exceptions. One of the best examples of the Establishment refusing to admit that it was wrong was the case of Timothy Evans who was hanged for the murder of his daughter Geraldine when in actual fact it was John Christie who committed the murder. Before Evans went to the gallows there was a lot of public disquiet about the verdict and even a petition to the Home Secretary but all to no avail, the conviction was deemed to be 'safe' by the Home Secretary and he was hanged in March 1950. In June 1953 Christie admitted killing both

51

Geraldine and her mother, Beryl. Even then there was no response from the government. MPs of the calibre of Michael Foot and Anthony Wedgewood Benn spoke for Evans but to no effect. In 1955 Michael Eddowes wrote a book *'The Man on Your Conscience'* in which he exposed the faults of the Crown's case and still nothing was done. In 1961 Ludovic Kennedy wrote *'Ten Rillington Place'* in which he gave a very convincing argument that Christie was insane and to all intents and purposes proved that Timothy Evans was innocent. The same year the Home Secretary R. A. Butler totally refused a request to have a second enquiry. In fact the Evans family had to wait till 1966 when Mrs Justice Brabin carried out a 14 month inquiry [costing the taxpayer millions] which actually concluded that Evans only 'probably' did not murder his baby but may have murdered his wife. So her conclusion was that he was hanged for the wrong murder. On the back of this the Home Secretary Roy Jenkins gave Evans a 'free pardon'. So at the end of the day the State, after 16 years, the expenditure of millions, evidence from two well researched books, an admission by the real killer, and in the face overwhelming public opinion, still refused to admit that it was wrong. It found a face-saving solution and issued a 'pardon' but the big question is how can you be pardoned if you have done nothing wrong? Here a total miscarriage of justice took 16 years of public hectoring to be half-heartedly acknowledged and a judge who should have been totally impartial gave the Crown a way out which was really a whitewash. She still carried on being a judge although her judgement should have been questioned. 'Pardon' is really quite the wrong word to use, and 'exonerate' would be more correct, but that would definitely infer a mistake on the part of the Crown, and for Crown read Establishment. There have, of course, been countless other cases both before and since then including The Birmingham Four who would undoubtedly have been hanged had hanging still been in force having wrongly been found guilty.

Governments are, of course, the greatest wasters of public money known to man. Whatever they say about being thrifty with the taxpayer's money is all hot air. They spend it as fast as they get it and always want more. They preach cost cutting, saving, and efficiency, but overall a government is probably one of the most inefficient and wasteful organisations going. Businesses run on the same lines would go bust very quickly. All the different departments of government are empire-builders. They all want more money and fight each other every year for a bigger share of the cake whether they need it or not. If they get it and do not need it they will spend it anyway. Unlike businesses they do not actually have to make the money, only to ask for it, therefore feel free to spend, spend, spend. The National Audit Office used to be a feared organisation for it is supposed to keep an eye on spending and point out unnecessary wastage, but of late it seems to have lost a lot of its teeth and these days contents itself with tamely pointing out the obvious, and being ignored by ministers. One of the greatest ways government wastes money is in daft projects which either never get started but on which millions get spent on preparation, or are started and then abandoned and quietly shelved - often in such a way that it takes investigative journalists months of work to trace. Every year our government commissions incredibly expensive reports on schemes that it may have promised. These reports often represent delaying tactics because by the time they actually get published the world has moved on, the original scheme forgotten, and leaving the report archived to gather dust. Companies which prepare these reports on, say, the environmental implications of some project or other, usually do a good job and, of course, are very well paid. They have vast filing areas for copies of all these unused reports and must actually get quite frustrated to see their months of hard work just shelved.

British politics, which once had a name for incorruptibility, is today, at the very least, tinged with corruption. At government level it is quite hard to be openly corrupt as there are safeguards, inspection procedures and committees to oversee MPs' every move but it does still happen. However, at local government level corruption is rife as is revealed in the Rotten Boroughs section of *Private Eye*. This reports corruption in local government in every issue yet the parties whose members sin seldom seem to do anything about it. Councillors appear to get away with all manner of misdemeanours and carry on in office. It beggars belief that when it comes to local election time these miscreants still get voted back into power, sometimes even after they have been prosecuted. The very low turnout at these elections may have something to do with this but it is nonetheless strange. It seems that it is at this level that large amounts of taxpayer's money is wasted on frivolities, or is squirreled away in pure corruption. One of the favourite ways of enjoying taxpayer's money is using it to go on foreign jaunts in the name of research that will supposedly do something to help with local governance. A spurious excuse at the best of times! You can learn all you need to about anywhere else through the internet, a book or even on the telephone. If this were to happen on the continent there would be immediate enquiries and the perpetrators would be out of office in a flash. Featherbrained schemes, ridiculous court cases usually trying to defend the indefensible, unwanted building projects, unrecoverable loans to dodgy friends or companies - the list could go on - but in the end it is the long-suffering taxpayer who foots the bill and is asked for more, year on year.

During the 19th century most politicians, including those at local level, came from the wealthy classes. Inevitably the working class could not afford to give their time because in those days political activity was all unpaid. There was little or no corruption on two counts. The first was that there was no need to be corrupt, the participants were wealthy enough. The second and probably the most important was the fact that shame was still a potent force in society. The loss of honour and standing connected with any impropriety with money was so great that it ruined people, and often their families as well, for life. This seems to have disappeared from public life today. Politicians at all levels do view the job as a gravy train, which it is, and a very lucrative one for many. No matter what they do wrong they will try to brazen it out and hang on to office. Certainly at local government level it seems quite difficult to attract people of honour. This is not an argument in favour of going back to the days of being governed by the rich and the landed gentry, but it does beg the question as to how do you get rid of unscrupulous, selfish and corrupt politicians, all of whom seem blessed with the gift of the gab. Attracting people of honour and integrity into politics these days is difficult. The power that political office gives people is a huge temptation, especially for the dishonourable.

RANT 4: ON FREEDOM

A dictionary definition states that 'Freedom is the quality or state of being free, especially to enjoy political and civil liberties'. These liberties have been hard won and should not be given up easily, yet in Britain today that is the way it seems to be going. 'Freedom' was the shout of every revolutionary leader in the past although in most cases it was their version of freedom, and not necessarily that of the populace. Leaders like to think that they can persuade people to believe in their version of freedom but invariably end up forcing not only their followers but everybody else to see it their way. Robespierre and Lenin were both good examples of this. Like most revolutionaries they believed in their virtuosity and 'knew' that they were the sole custodians of 'right' but in the end they had to force people to believe that they were. Like all revolutionaries they spouted freedom but ended up enslaving the people. Two quotes from Robespierre amply illustrate this: 'Any law which violates the inalienable rights of man is essentially unjust and tyrannical; it is not a law at all.' This was said before he came into power. Then: 'Intimidation without virtue is disastrous; virtue without intimidation is powerless.' And from Lenin: 'Liberty is precious – so precious it must be rationed.'

Freedoms in Britain have been won over a long period of attrition against the old nobility and gentry, though there was a small revolution, the Civil War, and it has taken a long time to get to where we are today. Whilst we cannot call the former Prime Minister Tony Blair a revolutionary, when he came to power he was in favour of 'new' and 'freedom from the old' and 'liberty'. He even renamed the party 'New' Labour. He certainly was elected on a wave of expectancy that the old humdrum and corrupt politics of the previous administration would change. However, during his stewardship he managed to introduce many cases of restrictive legislation, always in the name of liberty, or of safety for the general public. He was a very convincing man and his argument that if you have nothing to hide you have nothing to fear always seemed to get a sympathetic ear. He usually sought to assure everybody that the police would never abuse the extra powers that they were being given, though they always do. Our hard-won freedoms are rapidly disappearing and most people cannot see this. Britain had for a long time been way ahead of the rest of Europe when it came to granting the people 'freedoms' but the tables are turning. British freedoms are being eroded whereas in Europe they are not. Travel through the Netherlands, France, Italy and Spain and you see no sign of the intrusive CCTV cameras and there certainly are not the invasive bits of legislation that allow officials into houses and police to stop and arrest people without suspicion. Britain is certainly being taught what 'freedom' now means and with so many spin doctors surrounding him it is not surprising that Tony Blair managed to get his way, no matter how harmful the outcome was to the country, or more specifically to the individual.

RANT 5: ON THE FRAGILITY OF PERSONAL RIGHTS

There was a time, in recent history, really up to the First World War, when it was anathema for governments to intervene in personal lives or in the business world. People had to make their own way in life and at work and that meant making decisions. For some this was easier than others and if you fell by the wayside life was rough and tough and it really was. You had to rely on charity handouts or family support and probably worst of all, the workhouse. The big problem was that you were viewed as a failure and the people who dished out the charity were in actual fact never very charitable. Although the money may have been there to help those in need, the guardians hated parting with it so everything was made as difficult as possible. If all else failed you were sent to the workhouse where, in theory, the whole family worked for their food until they found a job and could feed themselves. The facts were very different. Most inmates were extremely badly treated and fed starvation rations which were halved at the slightest perceived misdemeanour. Families were always split and children as young as three were put to work and beaten if they didn't. Looking at it from today's perspective it was harsh, but at the time that was the way it was and people got on with life and the vast majority not only survived but made a living. However, life was hard for the poor, justice was burdensome to say the least, the employers had all the rights, and the ruling Establishment kept a tight grip on everybody except themselves. We have moved on since then. During the 20th century there was a gradual lessening of the harshness of the law, and personal rights have slowly got better with a proportional decrease in the power of the ruling classes. These freedoms probably reached their zenith between the 30s and 50s, excepting the war period. By the 60s the ruling class had seen a big change in its make-up. Parliament comprised a predominantly new class, one that had never before

59

tasted the heady heights of power. Since then they have become the Establishment and have been making their mark on society by way of a surreptitious form of centralisation and surveillance. In the last decades of the 20th century this has become repugnant but has been allowed to happen with the aid of technology. With this has come a creeping loss of personal freedom. Because it is such a slow process and the politicians always put it across as being good for 'the people', the general public does not realise just how invidious this loss actually is.

Since New Labour came to power in 1997 they have managed to add to the number of criminal offences on the statute book by about 700. This is an incredible increase in the legislation governing our lives. On top of this the government has a win-win clause which states that ignorance of the law is no excuse for breaking it. To know the law in its entirety is an actual impossibility. The gradual increase in the power of the state and its servants is relentless. Whilst it can be said that the whole panoply of state bureaucracy and all its departments are the servants of the government [actually what they should remember is that they are the servants of the people], they all seem to have a wish to increase their powers, but the main arm of this stealthy growth in authority is the police force. The police as a force was started in London by the Peel government in 1829. It took over from the Bow Street Runners. In 1856 the system was introduced throughout the country, based on counties. Today there are 56 autonomous forces and although they do help each other when asked, there is a rivalry which often impedes their efficiency. In those early 'days their powers were very limited. However, year-on-year since then they have demanded more powers from parliament on the basis of an ever increasing crime rate. They nearly always get what they want and yet the crime rate keeps going up. The conclusion must be, therefore, that giving in to police requests actually does nothing to stop crime. Yet it is a guaranteed vote-catcher when a party fighting an election states it will increase police numbers and powers. You have to wonder why this should be. Could it be that the bigger the police force becomes the more inefficient it gets? It is a body that never gets an overall general audit on its efficiency because it is split into so many different units. Because they are so fiercely independent, any talk of amalgamation in order, perhaps, to make them more efficient, is always rubbished by the chief constables. They spend inordinate amounts of time and money on the appearance of being busy, but in fact little seems to get done. This is a generalisation for there are some police forces, many individuals, and some departments within different forces that are super-efficient and do excellent work. However, the generalisation is legitimate for if you stand back and take an overview of the whole force it does not seem very effective. Furthermore, every year both politicians and the heads of the constabulary swear that crime has reduced and always produce good percentages to back their words up. In actual fact, if crime had gone down by the amounts claimed over the past ten years then Britain would, today, be fairly crime-free.

If we go back to the 1950s the police generally walked the beat, they had their own patches which they knew inside out, and it seems they were able to keep far better order than they do today. The old bobby on the beat was a far friendlier character than many in the force today and would actually take time to stop and talk. On that basis he was far more able to elicit help and glean intelligence from the locals which is really an essential part of policing. If you alienate the people you are supposed to be looking after then it is difficult to persuade them to help you when you need it. It also has to be said that the police in the 50s and 60s were a pretty straight bunch of men. There is a perception, even if it is untrue, that corruption has crept into the force today. Another perceived or perhaps actual problem arises from the very low educational standards required to enter the police force. As the police acquire more power, and the law becomes more complicated, it is reasonable to assume that entry qualifications would go up perhaps to a basic minimum of five GCSEs. The opposite seems to be the case, because you can enter the police today having passed no exams whatsoever. In an age when education is so important and when life seems to get more tangled, as well as more restrictive by the day, it does not exactly fill the general public with confidence to learn that their policemen, whose word is 'the law', actually have no academic qualifications at all. This does not, of course, apply to all officers and there are plenty who do have an excellent education, but there are plenty who do not.

The general public may have been a lot more caring 30 years ago but the self-discipline that existed at the time seems to have gone out the window. It would, however, be difficult to blame the police or schools for this. The government, on the other hand, is culpable for sticking its nose so far into people's lives. However, it mostly has to do with parents and parenting. Discipline in children must first come from parents and if they cannot control their children it is very difficult to ask anyone else to do so. There are agencies that can help when needs must but in general people do not like asking because it is an admission of failure. But it is the primary duty of parents to teach their children the self-discipline and social skills which they need in order to live in society. This is necessarily somewhat simplistic. Most parents bring up their children incredibly well without any help and do not need sanctions such as physical punishment. However, there are many who do not have that ability, but in our nanny state where the government seems to want to interfere in every aspect of our lives, they have actually withdrawn from these parents many of the sanctions that are necessary to control their children. It is a bit rich for government to blame everything on parents. However, having done their best, if the child or youth then misbehaves, parents can call upon the aid of other agencies. Yet it seems that most parents of ill-behaved children prefer to blame everyone else for their problems and furthermore do not actually support the authorities, whether the school or police, or other agencies put there to help. This serves to reinforce the bad behaviour and the child stands a very good chance of growing into a yobbish youth, which in turn may well lead on to criminal behaviour. The state and its servants cannot combat this with any real hope of success, and only when parents do their job properly and take full responsibility for the actions of their children will the problem be solved. And here we return to education. It is only though education that these things can be changed, and inevitably this takes time. Hence, quick-fix knee-jerk reactions from government will never work and just end up being another waste of taxpayer's money. One way, perhaps, of helping this process is to include the parents in any charge brought against a child who has committed an offence. This does happen in other countries where it seems to be a real success. If parents know they will be charged along with their delinquent child it seems to have a salutary effect on how they look after that child.

The third form of control, and perhaps the most secretly pervasive, is the growth in the use of CCTV cameras. Britain already has more of this intrusive technology than any other country in Europe. Furthermore, there are plans afoot to install hundreds more cameras on the basis that they aid crime detection. This, they may or may not do, but they definitely seem to do nothing for crime prevention. The sad thing is that the most of the law abiding population 'who have nothing to hide' accept this further intrusion without complaint because it is said to 'help' the police. But this selfsame help is being used to spy on everyone and our privacy is being eroded much faster than we can possibly know or believe. People are filmed and watched 24 hours a day in control rooms and often by 'security men and women' who have very few, if any, educational qualifications and therefore work with limited initiative. These are precisely the type of people who do exactly as they are told, whether it is legal or not, and who have no qualms about snooping on others. These control rooms contain huge banks of screens and sophisticated surveillance equipment and really ought to be open to the public so it can be seen exactly what is going on. If that were the case, instead of them being well-hidden and secret, then the people might have a very different view as to their acceptability, or otherwise. Another very important question relating to these cameras is their cost. How much does a control room with 50 or 100 screens actually cost? What are the running costs? Has this ever been put to the electorate? After all, it is they who are paying one way or another, and the costs involved in equipping, staffing and maintaining these 'snooping rooms' must be enormous. Where does the money come from, central government or council taxes? This proves how underhand a government can be, for such detail, important as it is, has never been included in a manifesto or put to the public in any way whatsoever. Perhaps we no longer care about our personal freedoms and are quite happy to be spied upon all the time? It is certainly difficult to see the trend being reversed since none of the political parties state that they will dismantle the surveillance system. We do seem to be creeping towards the Orwellian vision of 1984 and no one seems to care. It is notable that when satellite dishes were first introduced the public needed planning permission to put one up but there is no mention made now of requiring consent for these intrusive instruments [which in fact we all love for the variety it brings to television] all over towns. Why is this? Might it have something to do with the fact that it will make it much easier one day just to have a little monitor added to the 'box' which can see everything that goes on within the house? This would be a relatively easy thing for a government to do and activate by stealth without any consultation as has already been the case with CCTV. Individual connection cards can already be targeted by television companies so

debate, the British media, have been fairly silent on the subject. It would, for example, be very easy for a government to insist that every new TV had a small camera in it. Digital technology makes this sort of thing much easier than it used to be with analogue. Already any home with a digital satellite system is linked directly to a vast computer system and should you fall foul of the provider for any reason your supply can instantly be stopped. This alone proves that we are already very close to having a 'spy in the house', and who is insisting that a digital system of broadcasting replaces analogue? The government, of course....

The present New Labour government proposes that we should all have ID cards using the argument that these are needed in the fight against terrorism. The big question 'HOW?' is never fully answered. How would ID cards have stopped the carnage of 9/11? All the perpetrators had passports which are supposedly even more effective than ID cards. How could ID cards possibly have stopped the last series of London bombings? They were all British boys from good families and most had degrees and professional jobs, and so all of them probably would have had ID cards and been quite prepared to show these to anyone who asked. The conclusion is that they have no effect whatsoever. The issue of ID cards has far more to do with the fact that at the time the Home Office minister David Blunket was a control freak. The government agreed with him, as of course did the police. They, along with other government agencies, anticipate a huge increase in their power over the general public through their introduction. ID cards have never been popular in the UK but government spin, linked to the current threat of terrorism, is definitely having a softening effect on public attitudes. More and more people seem to be willing to acquiesce to the government's demands. In fact it is going ahead with plans to introduce them at a cost of billions to the taxpayer and the opposition to this is minimal, even from other political parties. So it seems that everyone will soon be required to carry one at all times - no doubt with fairly severe penalties to back this up. Is this really what we want? ID cards are yet another means of general surveillance and control, and that is the top and bottom of it, but that precisely is what those people in power actually want. It really is a matter of such importance that it should be put to a referendum. The amount of money the whole scheme will cost to introduce and then run is obscene, whatever figure the government puts on it, and it is rising all the time and could double. Governments never admit to the real price of any of their hair-brained schemes for they know that there would be a public outcry. In fact, even when the project is completed it will be impossible to get accurate figures for no government would ever be prepared to admit how badly they had miscalculated and mislead the public. Another point here is do people realise just how much power this will give government officials, not merely the police? ID cards will have to be carried at all times, with no leaving it at home and producing it later, as with driving licences, and no excuses will be accepted. You will have to produce it on demand from any 'competent official', and the act legalising the cards will empower plenty of these. If you cannot provide the card instantly there will at the very least be an instant fine, or should the official wish, an actual arrest. Of course, once you are arrested your finger prints and DNA sample will be taken and you will feature on the national criminal database merely because you did not have your ID card with you. This is actually what both the government and the police want, i.e. everybody featured on the national DNA database. What they would really like is for a DNA sample to be taken from every child that is born and even this will happen if Britain carries on the way it is going. In actual fact, it has already been mooted by some senior police officers. It really is quite scary, for these measures would give the government unlimited powers and in the words of Lord Acton in the 19th century, 'power tends to corrupt and absolute power corrupts absolutely'. Governments are already incredibly secretive, power-hungry and fairly corrupt institutions in our liberal democracy, so there is no reason to doubt that they will take on and use any additional powers that they possibly can. Not only use, but misuse and abuse these, as they have already demonstrated with the misuse of the Terrorism Act.

There is already a bill going through Parliament which gives police the power to take samples of DNA and blood, and to test for drugs prior to a person being charged. We are assured that these powers will only be used should the police have reasonable suspicions. Then there is a proposal to allow police to arrest anyone whom they suspect of committing any crime. Again we are assured by politicians that these powers will not be abused. However, looking at the police record on abuse of power, it is a safe bet that this will happen and be used against innocent people, and for the most minor offences. Imagine as a scenario that of being arrested and having a DNA sample taken for simply dropping a sweet paper in the street. This is possible, and current and planned laws will allow this. A classic case of total abuse of power involved an old gentleman named Walter Wolfgang who was bundled out of 'people friendly' New Labour's annual party conference in 2005 for shouting 'rubbish' at foreign secretary Jack Straw. His removal was undertaken in full view of TV cameras by a group of huge, dark-suited security men who looked more like pub door bouncers, and certainly acted with similar alacrity. Why on earth does a political party at conference need such bullies? To throw the old man out revealed a complete absence of any form of freedom of speech, and not only that, but a young man sitting next to him went to his aid and he too was thrown out roughly. Second, it proves that we are moving towards a police state. Gone are the halcyon days of the 70s when deputy leader George Brown, and even prime minister Harold Wilson, would simply argue back at hecklers. However, when Mr Wolfgang [who was a fully paid up member of the Labour Party], tried to return to the conference, which was his right, he was then arrested under the Terrorism Act. How can the police or the politicians justify that? We are continually being assured by the prime minister that such stringent powers will only ever be used against the people for whom they are intended. And yet here at the party conference, itself with the prime minister in attendance, together with the whole hierarchy of New Labour, we have a blatant abuse of the Terrorism Act against an elderly gentleman. Perhaps we may be permitted to ask whether the arresting officer was so ignorant that he could not distinguish between a terrorist and an amiable old man. The politicians were quick to see their mistake and apologised, but there was nothing forthcoming from the police. Such violations of our hard-won freedoms happen on a daily basis and the powers that be get away with it. Both government and the police, and for that matter most government agencies with power over us, will always abuse their given powers because that is in the very nature of these beasts. The big problem with giving these people so much power is that they do not exactly have the initiative or common sense to go with it, and yet we are asked all the time to trust the government. Is it any wonder that so many people do not?

A good insight into the 'nanny state', which, incidentally its creators, the politicians, constantly deny is in fact happening, lies with the health and safety legislation. This is used and abused on a daily basis by the Health and Safety Executive, councils, and the police, all of whom harass people over the most trivial of things. Often such legislation is brought in to protect people from big multi-national companies from whom protection may indeed be needed, but inevitably it is used against the small man for he is an easier target and the big fish continue to get away with it. Britain has definitely reached the point where health and safety legislation is such that it is burdensome and is abused. It also appears to deny people the right to take responsibility for their actions, or even to think for themselves, so much so that they seem to be losing that ability. A simple recent example involved a group of builders laying the foundations for a bungalow. They were not wearing hard hats as there was no structure around higher than their ankles. A health & safety officer came by and demanded that they all wear hard hats. Following the mild protests that ensued he threatened to close the site down. Another instance of such sheer lunacy occurred in a British Transport office in London. A manager there had to produce a monthly report for the Health & Safety Executive but this proved difficult as there really were no hazards in the office; it was just a normal office. Or that is what he thought, because following a health & safety inspection it was found that there was in fact a serious hazard which should be included in the report. And the hazard? - The Tippex and the Tippex diluting fluid. As a result, from then on every month the amount of this dangerous substance that was used had to be mentioned in the report. Clearly, legislation should never replace 'common sense' and it is a precious commodity which, in fact, most small firms have, and this is far better than all the legislation in the world! What health & safety legislation in fact does is to inhibit efficiency and a lot of the smooth running of small businesses. The government, invariably backed by the unions and various departments, keeps adding to legislation and then appoints thousands of inspectors to go round and harass businesses. Education and common sense are far better resources in life than intrusive legislation. It is utterly preposterous, for example, that people actually suggest that 'no smoking' legislation be extended to private houses. How on earth could that be enforced - short of having people come into your house with smoke detectors or having family members snitch on each other and leading to prosecutions? Unless, that is, 'the box' is watching you. Is this the sort of world in which we want to live? The very people who suggest this sort of thing should really take a close look at their own motives. They are the type of people who flourished under Stalinist regimes. The very

70

thought is outrageous and really begs the question as to how these people get into the positions of power where they feel that they can make such loony suggestions. Another totally daft proposal that may well actually come into being is the banning of junk food adverts before a certain time each evening. Why not ban them altogether on the grounds that banning anything you don't like seems to be the trend! What all these bans reveal is the total collapse of decent education. Educate people properly, and especially to think for themselves, and to know what is good and what is bad for them, and the outcome will be far more satisfactory than all that achieved by officious and meddlesome legislation. If, when it comes to eating, they decide to ignore the advice then that is their decision and does not require do-gooder busybodies to interfere. In Tony Blair's words, 'education, education, education' is the only answer, but to be effective it must be education of the kind that makes people think for themselves, and not leave them thinking that authority should do their thinking for them.

Marriage is another area in which government has interfered to the great detriment of the institution. Everyone agrees that the stable family relationship of a mother and father is the very best way of ensuring the correct nurture and upbringing of children. Until the 70s and 80s this was the norm. Subsequently governments have done everything that they can to facilitate the easy break-up of the family unit. Those tax benefits and allowances that were given to married couples, and arguably helped keep families together, have been abolished mainly to the benefit of the treasury. Divorce has been made so easy that now it is just a matter of course. Equal rights are given to co-habiting couples which also make it very easy to split up and this is happening on an ever-increasing basis and often without much thought for the welfare of the children. This inevitably results in distressed children who develop social and psychological problems, and which in turn often leads to their bad behaviour. This results in politicians standing back and wringing their hands and stating that 'families aren't what they used to be', and pondering deeply over what should be done about it. They consequently also make fatuous, pointless and often patronising suggestions as to how to strengthen the family, yet it is they who are most responsible for this disastrous state of affairs. The family unit is all-important in society. Moral traditions within society come down through the family, and because during the last 50 years family bonds have been weakened so much by politicians, then this pattern is no longer being maintained. This can be seen by a study of societies where family bonds remain strong, for example in France, Italy and Spain. In each of these countries family ties are still robust and these seem to pass on a sense of family well-being and greater self-discipline than appears to be the case in Britain. Schoolchildren in general in these countries are well behaved both in and out of school, and there are certainly plenty of areas where crime is almost unknown. They seem to be happier, more stable people, and their children are polite and respectful.

Another idiosyncrasy of government that never ceases to amaze is the way that they dish out ministries. When the prime minister hands out these positions he does this on the basis of those who have helped him most. They receive the best jobs, whilst people who helped him least get the least important. What seldom happens is that the person most suited to a particular post actually gets that job. For example, how often in the last 20 years or so has a farmer or even anyone who knows anything about farming been in charge of the Ministry of Agriculture? Instead we have a lawyer or an accountant or another similar professional at the head of the farming industry. Why should he know anything about it or be bothered to learn about it? He has a ministry full of civil servants to give advice, and no doubt he relies on them. Of course, none of these have ever worked on a farm and few, if any, have qualifications in agriculture and so the best advice he is getting has every chance of being well off the mark. Unfortunately this has been much the case in farming over the last 30 or 40 years. So much so that Britain, which ought to be able to feed itself, instead imports two thirds of its food. British agriculture has been decimated by the sheer idiocy of the ministers supposedly in charge. If you want good examples of how countries can be supportive of its farmers, you just have to look at France, the Netherlands, or even Germany.

When was the last time an educationalist was in charge of the education system, or a doctor or medical man in charge of the health service? Is it any wonder that ministers therefore make errors? Often they are not up to the job but have been given it on the basis of their loyalty. When eventually they are sacked, as sometimes happens, it causes ill-feeling or they are ennobled and end their days sitting in the House of Lords, still being well-remunerated for their time [as long as it is designated, 'expenses']. The worst thing about this system is that you never have an overall view of the situation, and long- term planning seems to be totally out of the question because each new minister wants to put his mark on the subject. Hence, an assessment of just about any ministry over the past 20 years suggests little else but muddle, constant change and the vast waste of precious resources to the detriment of the long-suffering taxpayer.

RANT 6:   ON INTER-GOVERNMENTAL RELATIONS AND THE 'SPECIAL RELATIONSHIP'

Another sweeping statement, but one that is generally valid, no matter how friendly countries appear to be or even ought to be because of treaties that they have between them, self interest will always win out. During the Second World War the phrase 'special relationship' was coined by Winston Churchill to describe the friendship between Britain and America. This was based on the British role in the birth of America, and because both countries spoke English and was used despite the fact that although America did not enter the war immediately, they did not approve of Hitler. At the time Britain desperately needed American help for the war effort so there was a fair bit of sucking-up involved, for although the relationship between Roosevelt and Churchill did become quite close, at first Roosevelt was not at all sure about the British prime minister. All these things were basically true, but, and this was a big BUT, the Americans were jealous of British power and global influence, both economic, and political, and really disliked their Empire. This had nothing, or not much, to do with the stated reasons of freedom, democracy and anti-colonialism etc., but because of the trading power and political influence it gave Britain, and also the fact that at the time the pound sterling was used world-wide as a valuation benchmark and general currency, as opposed to the US dollar, and this gave Britain certain trading advantages. Consequently, in all negotiations that Churchill held with Roosevelt on the topic of the war there was, in fact, a hidden agenda on the American side. This was to lessen Britain's prestige throughout the world and to replace it with its own, and, in fact, to bankrupt the country if it could. This America succeeded in doing quite successfully. At the first meeting between the two leaders in 1941,

75

and long before the United States entered the war, Churchill was pressing Roosevelt for badly-needed aid to help the war effort. This was refused and really America would have been quite happy to see Britain defeated by Germany because this would have brought about a huge change in the balance of world power to the great advantage of the United States. However, when Britain started making concessions on trade such as allowing the United States to do business in areas of the Empire which had hitherto been closed to them, things began to change. Roosevelt also extracted a promise from Churchill that Britain would give colonies of the Empire their freedom following the end of the war. Again it should be emphasised that this had nothing to do with freedom or democracy and instead everything to do with trade and global influence. This then was the context in which the 'special relationship' was to begin. From then on Britain received the war supplies that she desperately needed but everything she did receive from the US was charged for, and there were no concessions. The rest of Europe was handed massive aid which was in the main, free from America [although it was always in their own interests] but Britain had to pay for every single resource. Before the war half of the businesses in the US were British-owned, but at the end the bill was so great that America was able literally to asset-strip Britain, and the value of British-owned businesses in that country went down almost to nil. Whilst aid was flowing freely during the war, the day it ended so also did the aid. This came as a bit of a shock to the politicians who had expected it to continue for a while at least, but it did not. In panic the economist Keynes was sent to the United States with cap in hand. He really thought that he could persuade the administration to cough up. In fact, all that he managed to do was rub everyone up the wrong way and eventually returned to England with his tail between his legs. After a great deal of discussion, and even some pleading, the Americans did agree a five billion dollar loan which saved the day but every cent had to be paid back, all of it with

76

interest. The total debt was not actually paid off until 2006. At the time this contributed to the virtual collapse of the British economy and in turn also helped to end the Empire. Most people would accept that the latter was not a bad thing, especially as it was, in any case, unsupportable. However, the point is that the 'special relationship' between Britain and America was, and is today, and always will be all one-way. The war had cost Britain so dearly that the US held all the cards and everything that they could do to damage the British economy and its influence in the world they did, and they did so both with malevolence and success.

Since the Second World War the US has flexed its muscles increasingly and let everyone know just who is the boss but in the most hypocritical way possible. It is probably fair to say that all governments are somewhat hypocritical, which is why they all have secrets and which despite Freedom of Information Acts they still refuse to divulge. However, the American government really does go over the top. It preaches democracy and human rights and yet since the war has supported numerous dictators throughout the world, notably in Latin America and the Caribbean Islands, some of them pretty brutal types. But they have been kept in power and aided so long as they supported the American line, and that usually means allowing American businesses to run each country's economy. Batista in Cuba was a classic example of this. He was an odious dictator and whilst in power let American business pervade the whole of the country. Cuba was, in fact, used literally as a rest and recreation base for Americans. When Castro threw him out and then fell out with the United States over the nationalisation of their businesses they declared war on him and Cuba has suffered sanctions ever since. There were also numerous CIA plots to overthrow the government and to assassinate Castro himself, all incredibly inept because he was still there after nearly 50 years.

The converse happened in Chile where the people elected Allende as president. He was supposedly a Marxist and this is how the American propaganda machine has described him, but most learned opinion points to him being a socialist. However, the United States portrayed him as a communist and were not prepared to put up with a communist 'at their back door'. What he did not do was to accept the American line and committed the ultimate sin of nationalising some American-owned businesses. Within three years there had been an internal coup [widely recognised as having CIA complicity], and he was replaced by a ruthless dictator in the form of General Pinochet. He allowed American businesses back into Chile and although the United States made the odd little noise about 'dictators' and 'human rights', they were quite prepared to let him rule without interference from the CIA which he did for 15 fairly brutal and chaotic years, until eventually the majority 'will' and his age forced him out of office. During his dictatorship thousands of people went missing without trace and many more were imprisoned and tortured. Many harrowing stories emerged during those years, but so long as trade flourished the United States kept quiet.

Two recent examples of American invasions planned in order to get their own way are those of Grenada in 1983, and Iraq in 2003. Both had fairly disagreeable ruling dictators but neither liked America. It should be mentioned that neither actually posed a threat to the United States but in both instances that was the excuse which justified the intervention. In the case of Grenada it seems absolutely ludicrous to claim that this tiny island with a population of 92,000 could in any way be a threat to the mighty US of A. What the Reagan administration at the time claimed was that an airport being built with the aid of the Cubans could be used for military purposes. Here, too, is an example of the 'special relationship'. Grenada is part of the British Commonwealth and technically, or even legally, a monarchy with the Queen as head of state, and therefore in a British sphere of influence. You would assume that as a matter of diplomacy, if not courtesy, the Americans would let the British government know what they were about to do, particularly as there was a very pro- American prime minister in office in the form of Margaret Thatcher who actually got on very well with President Reagan. However, when Reagan decided to invade he did so in complete secrecy. Even the media was not allowed in. As usual there was international condemnation from the United Nations down, and even Thatcher expressed 'surprise' which could be taken as a mild form of criticism. Reagan made excuses but in the end, that is all they were and in any case he ignored it all and, as always, within a few months the world had move on and the case of little Grenada was forgotten. However, the United States got their way, with the Marxist Maurice Bishop overthrown, and trading relations restored. There were no repercussions, nor could there be, for who can stand up to the biggest economy in the world? Even the United Nations is totally handicapped because the US pays most of its costs and without this support it could not function.

In order to invade Iraq the US desperately needed at least one ally and so suddenly the 'special relationship' was revived. Here the United States used Britain to help persuade others to join in the toppling of Iraq President, Saddam Hussein. All the old excuses were rolled out, for instance, that Iraq was a real threat to the rest of the world, and especially America. It was said that they had weapons of mass destruction, which they didn't, that they harboured terrorists, especially al-Qa'eda, which they didn't, and so on. The two governments then set about legitimising their objectives by trying to get the UN to sanction an invasion but when that didn't work they went ahead nevertheless on the pretext that an earlier UN resolution had permitted this. This was then hailed as a great success, and initially it was because the invasion itself and the overthrow of the regime was rapid and relatively bloodless.

Furthermore, the Iraqis, especially the residents of Baghdad, welcomed the invaders with open arms. After the initial jubilation, things began to fall apart. The first thing the American High Command did on entering Baghdad was to disband the local police force and Hussein's army. This left a gaping hole in the security of the city which the invaders could not fill mainly owing to their lack of knowledge of the Arabic language. The result was that the locals started looting offices, houses, museums and any building that had been vacated. As the days passed, law and order broke down completely and, in actual fact, the situation became an unmitigated disaster both for the US and British forces. The Iraqi people have not done too well either. They have suffered more since Hussein was overthrown than ever they did under his control. They lack fuel, water, electricity, and above all any form of security. And this, of course, is compounded by them having to live under an occupying force which is never liked even if it is supposedly benevolent. The longer that the occupation continues the more strident will the opposition become. Furthermore, because the invasion occurred in an unseemly hurry with no forward planning as to what to do with the country following the overthrow of the Iraqi government, the only answer in the short term has been military rule. No one ever likes that because it is always arbitrary and usually harsh. What the invading forces did was to demolish the whole structure of government. All authority, and especially that of the army and the police [which had been Hussein's muscle], was disbanded and sent home. This left not only a power vacuum which could not be filled overnight but also many very discontented fighting men who had been the best paid in the country and were now totally unemployed and unemployable, under the foreign military regime. It will inevitably take a long time to rebuild what was destroyed at a stroke. All this means that the occupying forces will be staying for years. The longer they remain the more resented they will be and the more personnel losses they will suffer. It does not seem to dawn on any of

against Britain in a UN Security Council vote and forced a humiliating and ignominious withdrawal. The rights or wrongs of the British actions in Suez are not for discussion here, but rather the one-sidedness of the 'special relationship', for Britain's weakness in the world was further displayed and her influence in the Middle East further damaged. This is presumably what the US wanted, for until that time British influence in the Arab world was far greater than theirs. When in December 1989 the US invaded Panama - supposedly because American citizens were being threatened [which did not actually stand up to close scrutiny] - not a peep was heard from the British government. However, this excuse alone shows the dishonesty of government statements for in actual fact the then administration of President Bush had fallen out with President Noriega of Panama whom they had helped to gain power in the first place. He had worked for the CIA but after assuming power with their help he became a nuisance and the administration wanted him out. Excuses were therefore made and American forces invaded. Noriega was captured, taken back to the United States, charged with drug offences and imprisoned for life. The sentence was a forgone conclusion and it is arguable as to whether actually he received a fair trial. The British government said nothing even though the invasion was totally illegal. These provide classic examples of the perfidy between so-called friendly nations, especially those claiming a 'special relationship'.

RANT 7: ON AMERICAN NATIONALISM

The CIA is internationally known as a law unto itself, often working without the knowledge of its own government. However, it is a supremely nationalistic organisation as well as being quite inefficient and naïve, and whilst pursuing the US national interest it has nevertheless made some of the biggest cock-ups in history. For example, in 1970 the US fell out with Prince Sihanouk of Cambodia who refused America entry into his country to search for the Viet Cong who were using Cambodia as a conduit to South Vietnam. So the CIA financially aided a coup. This was led by General Lon Nol who was both anti-communist and pro-America. Like most generals who seize power he was not a good ruler, and Cambodia, already an unstable country, started the inevitable and inexorable slide into chaos. Four years later and after countless bombing raids and incursions by the US, all of which did more to destabilise the country than stop the Viet Cong, the communist insurgents in the form of the Khmer Rouge, with Chinese aid, toppled the Lon Nol government. This in turn led to another four years of indescribable misery, torture and the death of a million innocent Cambodians and the total ruination of the country's economy and infrastructure. To cap this mistake, and by a thought process that is not only incredibly convoluted but verges on the side of lunacy, when Pol Pot and his savage regime were eventually overthrown with the aid of North Vietnam and with a far more sympathetic regime in place, the US refused to recognise it because of the North Vietnamese connection, and carried on claiming that the Khmer Rouge was still the legitimate government of Cambodia. All this happened in the name of US national interest and the fact that, arguably, the blame for the deaths of the million innocents carried out by the Khmer Rouge can be laid directly at the door of the United States never seems to be brought up by anyone, nor, indeed, the Americans themselves.

In the early 1960s Indonesia's President Sukarno was becoming far too close to communist Russia and in general was following an independent line as far as his country was concerned. Again this was seen as a threat to the US. Under CIA auspices the pro- American Suharto took over. The CIA then supplied him with a list of 200,000 names of supposed communists most of whom were rounded up over the period immediately following the takeover and nearly all of whom were murdered. No trials, just torture and execution. This too was done in the name of American interests. However, it literally can be said that the United States government, via its agents, was directly involved in the murder of these people and again no one ever mentions it. It is, of course, doubtful whether many Americans were ever aware of these incidents as they were not widely publicised in the US, nor probably, would they care had they been. If their government says an action is necessary for their safety, then they would go along with it, however dreadful. It is difficult to see how normal, rational people can possibly see the murder of thousands, or even millions of people, as being in their national interest, but it does happen. As long as it is not their own men being killed then the majority do not really care.

In 1975 a new Portuguese government granted Angola independence, and in the ensuing chaos made a hurried exit leaving the various nationalist factions to fight it out amongst themselves. The two main players were Agostinho Neto's Marxist Popular Front for the Liberation of Angola [MPLA] and Jonas Savimbi's western orientated UNITA. Needless to say Neto was supported by the USSR in the form of Cuban troops armed by Russia, and Savimbi by both the US and the Republic of South Africa. Savimbi was winning the battle until Cuban troops were ordered in by the USSR. The CIA covertly supported Savimbi for years and turned what might have been a quick victory and peace into a 20- year civil war which resulted in the deaths of probably two million people, most of whom were innocent civilians trying to get on with their lives. You could well ask, 'for what gain?', since after all the trials, tribulations and devastation of the civil war, Savimbi eventually came to a negotiated settlement and accepted a junior role in the Angolan government. Again the real losers were the common people who find life in these areas of Africa hard enough without the idiots in search of power - backed by the greater idiots of big powers - fighting over influence, and in the process devastating their lands and bringing their homes down around their ears.

CIA support for regimes that could harm individual Americans is not unknown. During the Vietnam War they encouraged and also gave active support to tribesmen in northern Laos in an attempt to cut off the Ho Chi Minh trail which the Viet Cong used in order to run arms to the south. The main price for this help was to turn a blind eye to their heroin industry. Additionally, they then helped to distribute the drug and this was targeted mainly at US soldiers in the south undertaking a bit of R & R. This actually started a serious drug problem amongst military personnel, especially GIs. Again by some acrobatic thinking this was allowed to go on in the name of national interest. Hundreds of lives were ruined by drug addiction and the price was obviously seen as worth it although the arms run was never stamped out and, of course, the United States lost the war. Had this been known to the general public at the time it seems likely that there would have been a national outcry but things like this are always kept well hidden from public scrutiny.

Examples of perfidy between nations are legion. These are often the direct result of personality clashes between leaders. It usually matters not a jot what the people think, or the prospects of damage, injury and death, because the leaders still whip up the support necessary for them to justify their actions. One of the best examples of pure duplicity was the Non-Aggression Pact planned in August 1939 between Hitler and Stalin, two of the most treacherous and dishonourable men that the world has ever produced. The treaty was signed in Moscow by the German foreign minister Joachim Von Ribbentrop and General Secretary Joseph Stalin and was ratified a week later. Hitler and Stalin were uneasy bedfellows although funnily enough they both had very similar ideas about how to run a country. It is an irony of history that although one was a fascist and the other a communist a close look at their ideas and methods reveals incredible similarities. Nevertheless they were, in fact, natural enemies and the treaty took the world by surprise. For Hitler the treaty was intended to buy time and to make sure that Stalin would not join the British against him. The price for this was a share in Poland. Hitler told Stalin that he was going to invade Poland and that when he did Stalin could move into the east and himself annex a big chunk of that country. This was pure brinkmanship by Hitler for he had every intention of invading and conquering the whole of Russia as soon as he could. Stalin did not actually believe or trust Hitler but he too needed time to bolster his military strength. However, Stalin did believe that Hitler would honour the treaty, at least in the foreseeable future. Stalin took Hitler at his word even though he was warned by Churchill that there was mounting evidence that Hitler was going to invade Russia. He ignored the warnings with the most dire and disastrous consequences for his country. This really was a classic example of chicanery of the highest order between two leaders. They signed a 'friendship pact' knowing that they would, one day, confront one another. This 'pact' actually led to a great deal of rejoicing amongst their respective peoples for neither particularly relished a war between the two countries. Little did the deluded populations realise what their immensely popular, but totally treacherous and deceitful leaders, had in store for them.

A more recent example of double standards in the context of the transatlantic 'special relationship' was American support for the IRA. If ever there was a terrorist organisation with a truly long, disreputable and even contemptible history [depending, of course, on which side of the Irish Sea you come from], it is the IRA. They bombed their way through the 70s, 80s, and on into the 90s with the tacit approval, and even the financial and moral support, of the American people and its government. Even when the IRA nearly managed to obliterate the British government by bombing their Brighton hotel in October 1984, the American government remained silent and carried on supporting the IRA and allowed large amounts of cash to be donated to their cause. This arose through a totally misplaced sense of helping the underdog against a repressive government, even though the government concerned was supposedly their best ally, and indeed had, in the beginning, been called in to protect the Roman Catholics. Successive US presidents have welcomed into the White House, and feted, the leaders of the IRA [in the guise of Sinn Fein, the IRA's political wing] all of whom were known to be commanders of the organisation. They did this in total disregard of any protest or representation made to them by their 'big ally', the British government. However, the instant that 9/11 happened the US government made it perfectly clear that everyone was either with them, or against them, in the war on terrorism. They still, however, could not find it in their hearts to place the IRA on their list of terrorist organisations. The faithful British government immediately fell in line and when is was again mentioned tactfully that the IRA was a terrorist organisation the best that the American president could do was offer a slight snub to Sinn Fein by refusing to invite them to the White House for the St Patrick's day celebrations. Double standards, or what?

The sick thing about the American support for the IRA is that it was founded on naivety, ignorance and prejudice. Naivety, because many Americans, including educated ones, believe that British forces were occupying all of Ireland and that the Irish were fighting for their independence. This mainly owed to a lack of information via the US media or the educational system, plus the fact that it was not high on the list of American priorities. Ignorance, because the real facts were not put to the public and what little was known was through information distributed by various Irish groupings in the US, most of whom were fiercely nationalistic. Neither the British, nor the Northern Ireland government whilst it existed, ever did much to counter this propaganda so it was a one-way street for the nationalists. And prejudice, mainly because of the large proportion of Irish families in the United States, many of whom had done very well for themselves, had considerable political pull and gave vast amounts of money to the various political parties. There were, therefore, votes to be won or lost in supporting or banning the IRA.

Very few people, especially Americans, actually remember that when British troops were sent to Northern Ireland in August 1969 it was at the request of the Northern Ireland government and it was mainly to protect the Catholic population from the Protestants. It should be said at this stage that until the 60s the Catholic population of Northern Ireland were in the minority and were very heavily discriminated against throughout society. They did, therefore, have a genuine grievance as British citizens. However, they were not badly treated in the way that the American media had portrayed. In comparison, for example, to the way the Caucasian Americans treat their Native American population, the Catholic Irish in Northern Ireland lived 'the life of Riley'. The US government continually preaches human rights and freedom around the world yet their own back yard is characterised by discrimination, ill-treatment and even cruelty, yet no mention is ever made of the plight of these native people in the American media. Nor is it ever used as a stick by other governments to do any persuading in the way that the American government does.

RANT 8: ON US TREATMENT OF NATIVE AMERICANS

A dispassionate look at the way that the US government has treated native Americans over the past 150 years would reveal a catalogue of broken treaties and promises, treachery of the highest order in most of their dealings, and even massacres such as the infamous example at Wounded Knee where soldiers of the US army slaughtered not only men, but women, children and even babies with impunity. Never has there been an official apology for any of the wrongs committed, or even any sort of recognition that there had been any culpability. Indian-owned or 'promised land' has been whittled down to a few barren areas devoid of any sort of development potential and largely ignored by most, including the government and its agencies. The government has in the past, and really still does, try to kill off Indian culture and traditions. Missionaries were encouraged and like missionaries the world over they often did, and still do, more harm than good. Full of good intentions they moved in, notably after Wounded Knee, to proselytize, although they called it 'civilize', and did everything to crush what they saw as a barbaric culture. Even the children of Native Americans were taken away from their parents against their will and educated in boarding schools where they were not treated with Christian love and understanding, but with deprivation and often downright cruelty. What these 'brave souls' did was to overlook completely what was essentially a caring and civilized culture where families looked after themselves and each other. But because it appeared different and, of course, was not Christian, it had to be changed. Today the Bureau of Indian Affairs is still largely unsympathetic to the Indians themselves and to their culture. Apart from a few exceptions the Indians who are left, about two million out of an original population of probably ten million are today amongst the poorest people in the US and suffer from the highest unemployment, the greatest health problems, and most unfortunate of all, the lowest self-esteem. Any other country treating a part of its population the way that the Americans treat the Indians would very quickly come in for the attention and disapprobation of the incredibly self- righteous US administration. To this list can be added the plight of the Afro-Americans who until the 70s lived in a state of apartheid similar to, and as harsh as, that in South Africa until the fall of the white regime. They were badly treated, discriminated against, murdered with impunity, and were the subject of the attentions of one of the most racist organisations that the world has ever seen, namely the Ku Klux Klan which is still in existence. If it had not been for their fight-back which they could undertake because of their sheer numbers, there is no doubt that they too would still be downtrodden. However, they did fight back, and in general now do have equal rights, although the South remains quite a racist area and there is still some discrimination. In contrast, the American Indians have had the stuffing knocked out of them over the past 200 years by the whites and it is difficult to see how they can make a come-back. There are self-help organisations which are doing their best to keep their traditional way of life going and in some areas actually to revive it, but it is an uphill struggle and no help or recognition is received from the US government. With their low self-esteem it is actually easier to blend in with the rest of the population than to try and keep their own culture alive.

RANT 9:   ON THE REAL 'SPECIAL RELATIONSHIP'

If ever the Americans actually have had a 'special relationship' with anyone then it is with Israel. It does not seem to matter what the Israelis do to their Arab brethren, it is alright by the United States. It should be pointed out here, that in terms of the Middle East the Arabs and Israelis are brethren, and both inhabited what used to be called Palestine in relative peace and friendship for a thousand years before the Zionists seized it and announced the State of Israel. When they took control they forcibly evicted over a million Palestinian Arabs, often with great brutality, and appropriated their houses, land and businesses without any form of compensation and in reality turned a large proportion of the Palestinian nation into refugees. This was theft on a grand scale, pure and simple. Many of these people were well-off middle class business people who before the takeover had Jewish friends. They then found themselves in total penury and living in squalid refugee camps in Jordan, Lebanon or Egypt. Is it any wonder that they were, and still are bitter? To compound the tragedy, the Palestinians remaining in Israel with Israeli citizenship, have been treated as second-class citizens ever since, and they too are naturally quite resentful. In consequence of these injustices [which make those in Catholic Northern Ireland pale into insignificance], arose organisations like the PLO and Hammas, both of which could be compared to the IRA. They fight for what they see as their just rights. The members of these organisations are not all down-and-outs looking for a fight, nor rabid Islamists, and many are from good upright middle class families whose wealth was plundered by the Israelis in the same way as the wealth of the Jews in Germany was expropriated by the German government in the 1930s. They have what most sensible thinking people would see as just cause. However, these organisations were very quickly placed on the US list of terrorist organisations and the thought of a Hammas leader being welcomed at the White House would send cold shivers down the spine of any president, and most of the American public. Why should this be? Could it have anything to do with the massive Jewish vote in America that is comparable to that of the Irish? If a comparison were to be made between the IRA and Hammas, then the latter would come out almost smelling of roses. The IRA was a gangster organisation that feathered its own nest by robbing banks on both sides of the border, extracting protection money from businesses and murdering anyone who stood in their way. In contrast, Hammas collects funds rather than robs banks, helps the destitute, and opens and runs schools especially for the poor and orphaned. The western media are also very one-sided in their reporting of the troubles in Palestine. For every Israeli killed by the Palestinian 'terrorists', 25 Palestinians are killed by the Israelis, but the media seem to give the impression that it probably is always Israel that comes off worst and it is always Israel that seems to get the sympathy vote.

Whilst it cannot be denied that both at the time that Israel was created, and for the first 30 years of its existence it faced phenomenal odds and had to fight for survival, its subsequent behaviour towards the Palestinian Arabs, if looked at dispassionately, will reveal that Jewry in general has learned little from its own history. Throughout the ages the Jews have been persecuted wherever they have lived, except in America, although even there in the early days they were discriminated against. At the end of the Second World War, and after it was seen what the Germans had done to them, they had the sympathy of the world. Because of that the world actually did nothing to stop the birth of Israel although it could be judged as an illegal takeover of a country. Britain and the US undertook a lot of double deals promising both sides support and usually letting the Arabs down. Hence the Palestinian Arabs had a lot to be bitter about. As soon as they formed defence forces of any kind [such as Fatah and Hammas], they were labelled terrorists yet there was little condemnation of the Stern gang and the Irgun during their terrorist days against the British. These two organisations were formed in the 1930s expressly to fight for and deliver an Israeli state. During the British mandate of Palestine both the Irgun [literally meaning The National Military Organisation] and the Stern Gang [formed by Avraham Stern as a breakaway from Irgun and actually called the National Military Organisation in Israel] murdered both British personnel and any Jew whom they considered a collaborator. They raised money mainly through extortion and bank robberies, and used most of the methods utilised by terrorists today. Furthermore, members of the Irgun and the Stern Gang [such as Menachem Begin and Yitzhak Shamir] later became prime ministers of Israel and these same ex-terrorists then refused to talk to those Palestinians whom they deemed to be terrorists; double standards if ever there were. They were even accepted by American presidents without demure. Today the Israelis treat their Arab citizens as second-class and are totally arbitrary in respect of what they allow them to do. The Israeli blockade of Bethlehem, for example, has ruined that town's economy. They do this in the name of security for they believe that Bethlehem is the starting point of a lot of terrorist attacks on Israeli targets. This is not the whole truth and the Christian mayor of that city has done his best to get the road blocks and other hindrances to the tourist trade removed, but with little effect. Whilst Israelis call it security, the Palestinians call it strangulation of their trade, which in turn leads to unemployment and more unrest. The real agenda is more likely to be that the Israelis would actually prefer all Palestinians to leave so that they can expropriate more land. What better way of achieving this goal than by killing off all means of making a living, which is exactly what they are doing to the Palestinian populations in Israel and the West Bank? Whilst we all condemn massacres of innocent people, the condemnation is usually very one-sided. When there is a massacre carried out by the Arabs there is instant disapproval from the United States, and the West in general, and the United States always manages to get a vote of censure through the United Nations. In contrast, when the Israelis carry out massacres, which they call retaliation, and innocent women and children are killed, that is labelled the price of war. This happens on a regular basis, and whilst there may be some comment from the rest of the world, this is always half-hearted and couched in terms of restraint, whereas what both sides should be trying to do is bring about peace. The United States never introduces a motion condemning these killings which are always far in excess of the numbers killed in Israel. President Bush refused to speak to Yasser Arafat because of his terrorist links, yet he welcomed Prime Minister Sharon to the White House, conveniently forgetting that while he was foreign minister in the Israeli government he permitted the massacres of hundreds of innocent men, women and children in the notorious refugee camps of Sabra and Chatila in the Lebanon. This was murder on a grand scale, and seemed to be murder for murder's sake, and similar in many respects to the gassing of the Kurdish village of Halabja by Saddam Hussein. It can also be compared to the Nazi attitude towards the Jews, for the Palestinians, who were totally defenceless, were killed just because they were Palestinians. The Israelis protested their innocence and stated that they had nothing to do with it, but it was all done with their approval and had they wanted to stop it they could have. However, as far as they were concerned it was simply the annihilation of more Palestinians, so that was alright.

The Israeli blockade of the Gaza Strip in 2006 when one of their soldiers was kidnapped turned that godforsaken stretch of desert into the Arab version of the Warsaw ghetto. The bombing of infrastructure - including electricity and water, roads and bridges, plus the demolition of houses, - is very similar to the Nazi response to one of its soldiers being kidnapped or killed, i.e. totally over the top and equally unacceptable in what we like to think is a civilised world. The harassment of thousands of innocent people by causing sound barrier explosions during the night, by starving them of what we would call the basics of life [for they even restrict the passage of foodstuffs and medicines into the country] is exactly the sort of over-reaction that you would have expected from the Nazis. If the Israeli government really thinks it can achieve its ends by this massive use of force against a largely unarmed opponent then it ought really to look at the history of its own people and how badly they have been treated in the past. Resentment is the only thing that will come out of this sort of treatment and if the Arabs were in a position to do the same to the Israelis there would be screams of outrage from its citizens, always, of course, backed up by the United States. You could well ask the leaders in Israel what they think of group punishment because it has happened to them in the past. Making the whole population of Gaza city suffer for the deeds of a few, flies in the face of any sort of decency and should totally be condemned. Yet within a couple of weeks of this atrocious behaviour the world had moved on and there was no further mention of it. The Palestinians of the Gaza Strip are forgotten and left to lead their wretched lives with little help from the West. If it were the other way round no doubt there would be UN resolutions, talk of sanctions and massive donations of aid.

The sad thing is that were both sides to take a leaf out of Mahatma Ghandi's book, and to use peaceful protest instead of violence, then there would probably have been a settlement by now. The old adage of two wrongs not making a right applies really well here. Violence begets violence as is blatantly obvious in the Arab/Israeli conflict. Every time one side inflicts casualties on the other there is a revenge attack. Why can they not see that this has been tried before by many nations - notably the Germans during the Second World War - and it has never worked, nor will it ever. It really beggars belief that intelligent people cannot see this. If, for example, one side unilaterally gave up violence they would instantly get the sympathy of the rest of the world, and probably the support they needed to fight their case, but violence will never win and there will never be a just settlement whilst the battle continues. Here the West has been very one-sided in their support, or lack of it, for the Palestinians. When Hammas called a cease-fire in 2006 they did actually stop military action but Israel did not. With continuous Israeli incursions into Gaza they eventually gave up and resumed rocket attacks but there were no voices heard from the West in their support. Even were a peace settlement to be forced on the two sides [which is highly improbable] by the big powers, it will be an uneasy one involving too many unresolved and contentious issues to be lasting. What they need to concentrate upon is trade. Only trade and prosperity will bring peace. If the Israelis helped Bethlehem, as a small example, to become the richest little city around, then the terrorism supposedly emanating from there would disappear. The local population, workers and businessmen alike, would see to that because all that they want to do is live in peace and earn a decent living. Once achieved, they would not like this wealth and prosperity to be placed in jeopardy. By killing Palestinian trade, all that the Israelis in fact do, is to act as a recruiting agency for the extremists. The Israelis have proved that they can turn the desert into a garden that produces enough to feed themselves and also have a thriving export trade. They should be sharing this knowledge with the Palestinians and doing their best to convert both Gaza and the West Bank into really prosperous enclaves. This would not be a threat to the Israeli state nor to its trade. It would lift the whole area out of poverty, bring back the tourists, and additionally demonstrate to the world just how good are both the Arabs and Jews at trade. Furthermore, granting the Palestinians their own state would in no way be a threat to the Israeli state, and that, if granted in an

honour of the country or the sake of the religion, but such considerations never help and the people always pay dearly, and become poorer. Israel is reducing the Gaza to a rubble heap through the use of its massive military superiority. By killing, wounding, starving and mercilessly harassing the people of Gaza any victory gained will be Pyrrhic, if indeed any victory can ever come. The United States tries to appear to be bending over backwards to facilitate a settlement but in actual fact the Arabs view this as all one-sided [which it really is], and therefore have little faith in the outcome.

RANT 10: ON THE UNITED STATES AND TRADING

The United States is probably the most anti-communist country in the world. Ever since the Second World War America has ranted about the dangers of communism and done its utmost to contain the danger, the Cold War bears witness to this. Of course, if a country is an important trading partner, things can change. China, a communist country that has vilified America for decades now has introduced a major change in economic policy that means that American firms can gain access to what potentially is a vast market and, of course, a huge resource of incredibly cheap labour. Suddenly most of the vitriolic rhetoric between them has ceased. The Chinese government remains communist, and is still a one-party state that has no qualms about killing hundreds of unarmed and peacefully demonstrating students in Tiananmen Square who were only asking for democracy. It has one of the worst human rights records in the world, executes hundreds of people a year [charging their families for the bullets] and yet suddenly has become a bosom buddy of the United States. The fact is never mentioned that China illegally invaded Tibet and overthrew the government in October 1950 forcing the ruler, the Dalai Lama, to flee and has ruled there with brutality and perhaps even genocide ever since. Tibet is left to rot under Chinese tutelage whilst the Dalai Lama wanders the world trying to get support for his cause and is quietly brushed off by all the governments that he visits as something of an anachronism. The United States actually finds him an embarrassment because he is unelected, and although revered in his country the Americans find him 'a bit quaint'. Furthermore, Tibet is of no strategic use to America or anyone else for that matter, but the Chinese just want a bit more land. Now they are pursuing a policy of land grab that involves shipping in a multitude of Chinese so that eventually they will outnumber the Tibetans. The unelected regime in Peking, however, holds all the cards and so Tibet suffers as a colony and Tibetans have absolutely no say in anything to do with their own country. As far as the United States is concerned the less said about the Tibetans the better for to interfere too much could endanger trade relations with China. The last thing that they are going to do is rock the booming economic boat by bringing up thorny little problems like Tibet. In reality the United States enjoys trading with countries which are governed by strong regimes - which is why in the past they have supported so many dictators. Strong government keeps workers in order, wages down, manages messy things like unions, and can ban strikes. What better atmosphere for American firms [along with plenty of European ones] to set up manufacturing bases in China in order to produce cheap goods for sale expensively in America and, of course, Europe? This does not help employment in their own country but does that matter when the balance sheets of some of the biggest companies in the world are involved?

Illustrating the point on a much smaller scale, before Castro came to power in Cuba it was ruled by the brutish dictator Batista. He let the Americans do what they wanted and American businesses ran the whole economy to the detriment of the local population who provided cheap labour. Cuba was at this time a holiday resort for Americans and a source of sweated labour. Batista's police, well paid and trained by the Americans, kept the workers in order. At the beginning of 1959 Castro took power in a *coup d'état* and Batista fled. Castro's government was immediately recognised by most of the world, including the US, and for a while it seemed to the United States that one strong regime had replaced another and the *status quo* would just continue. However, Castro started nationalising American businesses, and doing so without compensation. To make matters worse American influence and advice was rejected. In the eyes of the United States government of the time this was a heinous crime and quite unacceptable. This has continued to be the case for every subsequent administration because the Cubans have never been forgiven. The United States imposed sanctions and insisted that all their allies did the same, and they have remained in force ever since. Although the rest of the world now basically ignores these, they have, along with other factors like communism, kept the Cuban economy from growing and left the population in a state of poverty. This is still done in the name of national security. Is Cuba really a threat to the US? If the consequences were not so serious to the Cuban people and their economy, then it would be a joke. The thought that this little island off the coast of America is a greater threat to that huge and powerful country than, say, is China, is laughable. But the US administration does not like its delicate nose pushed out of joint by such a lightweight.

There are many more examples of the American government supporting strong men in power when it is to their advantage. This arises usually in matters of trade but the long-standing bogey of communism has always been a good reason to move in. This invariably helped stimulate the arms trade, itself always a popular motive for Americans. South Vietnam, the Philippines, Chile, Venezuela, Kuwait, and Saudi Arabia were, or are, ruled by unelected heads of state but ones that are friendly, so that is alright. The minute that any of these steps out of line, there is guaranteed trouble from the US. On the other hand, when democracy works but the elections introduce governments which do not please the United States, then they either will not speak to them, like Hammas in Gaza, or they organise a *coup* as in the case of Allende in Chile. So when it comes to trade and national security the United States always feels it can do what it wants irrespective of world opinion, and as a general rule their own people support them. Only during times of conflict when the number of body bags starts mounting up does the American public get restive.

101

RANT 11: ON EDUCATION

Politicians are always spouting on about education for, after all, it is a political hot potato. However, when politicians interfere they invariably get it wrong. The problem with education is that everybody has experienced the system and therefore thinks that they know something about it. A good comment from Plato [*Laws*] that all politicians should memorise and take to heart is: 'so long as the young generation is, and continues to be, well brought up, our ship of state will have a fair voyage; otherwise the consequences are better left unspoken.' For 'well brought up' read 'properly and well-educated'. During the 1997 election campaign one of Tony Blair's war cries was 'education, education, education' and that certainly helped him get elected. However, a brief look at what has happened to education since New Labour came to power will reveal muddle and chaos throughout the system. Teachers are demoralised at having continual change thrown at them, and on top of this, paperwork and bureaucracy take more and more of their time. One of the first things that New Labour did was to abolish the grant system for higher education. In an age when the economy is supposedly doing well and billions can be spent on unpopular wars, nevertheless funding for education can still be cut. Some might say that this is a foolish mistake but in reality it is criminally insane. In the 60s and 70s when the country's economy was truly a shambles and generally in retreat, grants were readily available for higher education. Our future lies in education, and especially higher education, rather than in foreign escapades. The difference between what the country spends on 'defence' [which, to the contrary, actually includes a fair bit of aggression, e.g. Iraq,] and education in general, but especially higher education, is absolutely outrageous. Universities are being told to become more commercial and their direct grants from government are constantly being cut. This inevitably means changes to the range of courses that they offer, and usually for the worse. Courses that are least popular are cut, no matter how important they may be to the country, or to the economy. Hence you find that physics and chemistry attract too few students to make the courses pay and so they are taken off the syllabus, which is really not very clever. What the government spends in one month of the Iraq fiasco would pay for all the universities in the country for the same month. Whilst taxation in general has been going up at an unprecedented rate over the past few years the proportion spent on education seems to be going down. Even at the secondary level the government is encouraging business to become involved and this inevitably has a dumbing-down effect, quite apart from the fact that getting industry involved is not a safe way to fund education. If an academy is set up with help from a particular organisation or company, first, they will want their say in matters educational, and second, if they go bust then funds from that source suddenly disappear, and we all know that this can happen with no warning. So how does this help schools? Basic primary and secondary education throughout the world, and especially in the richer nations, is funded by the government. Taxes are paid in order that these essentials can be funded, and not diverted to crazy and ruinously expensive foreign fiascos. It seems that the more taxes we are asked to pay then the less we receive in return, and going into Iraq has given the British public nothing but sorrow.

In historical terms the fight for free education is relatively recent. Prior to the 1870 Education Act there existed two layers of education. The top layer, the old public schools, was for the nobility, landed gentry and even the *nouveau riche* merchants, and it was expensive. The next layer comprised the grammar schools which were mainly for the professional classes such as lawyers, doctors and the lower clergy and these were relatively expensive. Everyone else lost out, and in any case, the children of the poor were very quickly put to work, as early as five-years-old, in order to enhance the family income. The 1870 Education Act made it compulsory for everyone under the age of ten to attend school. It must be said that at this stage, school was seen as an instrument of class segregation and control, teaching children respect for their superiors, and where they stood within society. However, the Act did not give free education. A charge of nine pence a week was payable, which was a considerable sum. Free education did not appear until 1918, although in 1893 those parents who could not afford the fees were able to apply for free education. Not until 1876 were employers actually forbidden to employ children under the age of ten. The school leaving age was raised to 11 in 1893 and 12 in 1899. State education at this stage was basic, long, and harsh and there was no choice. Applying for free schooling involved going before a self-righteous parish committee that looked down upon all before it and hated handing out freebies. Also, as always after the acceptance of charity, it carried a stigma almost equivalent to that of being sent to the workhouse, for the money had to come from parish funds, and this was unpopular both with the wealthy parishioners and the less wealthy all of whom had to contribute.

Education is a great leveller, and once the poor started to read, the very system that was installed to keep them in their place in fact now gave them confidence, largely through reading newspapers and through the availability of books in public libraries. At the turn of the century the working class began to ask unpalatable questions of the classes above and to demand equal rights. Slowly at first, these were prised from the ruling classes largely through socialist organisations such as the unions and also the Labour Party which was founded in 1900. These were all seen as subversive by the ruling classes and efforts were made to put them down or ignore them. There was also the fact that at the end of the 19th century child labour was still seen as an essential part of the booming British economy and consequently the legislators [many of whom were industrial barons,] were certainly hesitant about getting rid of it. Furthermore, the politicians in those days genuinely disliked interfering in people's lives [unlike those of today] so unless a big noise was made about something, little changed. In many ways it was thanks to what we would disapprovingly call 'do-gooders', as well as the subversive associations and clubs [again mainly of a socialist character], that change was actually achieved.

One of the main problems with education is that its aims and ends are not in the hands of educationalists. It is the politicians who have the power in education, in contrast to other professions such as doctors, lawyers, or architects, all of whom have their own governing bodies. These are always made up of people from their own professions who have proved themselves to be worthy of the position. Of course because the government holds the purse-strings for education, they feel no need to give up their control. Teachers don't have this privilege although it was promised them as far back as the late- 19th century. The people who govern education are almost never from that profession, and because they are politicians they never really have either the knowledge, nor the will to do the right thing on its behalf. They usually work through sound-bites, or have knee-jerk reactions to what they perceive to be the public's demands, without knowing what the public's demands really are. We regularly hear from politicians that they have consulted both the public, and educationalists. Such claims should always be taken with a pinch of salt. Wide-ranging consultations seldom actually take place, and politicians make up their minds, and then try to justify their decisions, by publicly stating that they are consulting the people. In reality these consultations rarely involve a wide range of people and they are usually conducted involving a hand picked audience which the government knows will give the right answers.

The ministers may be very able people, and may have a sense of direction, but that seldom extends beyond the date of the next election. This process has been, and remains, fairly ruinous to an education system that ought to be planned for at least 25 years ahead. In the early 20th century when state education was just coming into its own, the teaching profession was regularly promised its own governing body but this never happened. The main reason is that the politicians dare not part with so much power when they are paying [forgetting, of course, that it is our money in the first place]. Installing an independent governing body, made up of educationalists, would have a far more beneficial effect on education. It would give a better overview of the direction education should take and how it could be organised without the current disruption that emanates from the Department of Education every time a new minister takes over, or a new political party comes to power. A governing body of educationalists would have the same effect on education as that of giving the Bank of England the right to set interest rates has had on the economy. That outcome removed instantly the interference of politicians on decisions that in general they could only make in a context that is political, rather than economic. This one, seemingly simple, move had an amazingly positive effect on the running of the economy. The decision took a great deal of courage for a politician because it removed a very powerful tool from his options. But a glance at the performance of the economy over the past 50 years will reveal swings from boom to bust and back again with politicians at the helm. Although they will try in the future to claim the credit for the economy's steady performance over the past 10 years it is really to the credit of the governors of Bank of England. A similar glance at education over the last half century shows similar highs and lows, although fewer of the former and plenty of the latter, and if you look at the number of changes introduced on the back of political ideology then it is no wonder that teachers opt out in their thousands, and that these are

107

always the best ones. They just cannot put up with such political interference in their profession.

The destruction of the grammar and secondary school system in the 70s in favour of comprehensives was a purely political decision, and although the system had been somewhat elitist the subsequent comprehensive system resulted in a general and steady dumbing-down of education. This has failed many children and the old system is gradually, and by other names, being reintroduced. It always was, and remains, a total nonsense to pretend that all children are the same and can all benefit from the same education. Children like the rest of us are individuals and are very different, with contrasting rates of development and comprehension, and to try and put such a mix into the same class and to teach them well is to put inordinate and unnecessary strain on teachers. However, this does not worry our political masters who, when asked about the failing system, will never admit that there is anything wrong, and say instead that teachers are doing a wonderful job, adding that the next lot of changes which 'are about to be introduced will improve the whole system and make teaching easier'. Unfortunately they never do, they just add to the turmoil with which teachers have to cope. The worst thing that has happened to schools over the last 30 years is the gradual reduction of any form of sanction against unruly children. When children misbehave they need to be punished, as are adults when they break the law. This is an essential part of learning. The problem is that no sanctions remain for the teacher to use and so discipline in schools is not what it used to be. One of the biggest problems is that parents often do not back up the teachers so children feel that they can get away with almost anything, and frequently do.

A general lack of respect for anything or for anybody is now commonplace in British society. This seems to include any form of authority but sadly also includes the environment in which we live,

108

other people's property, and even other people's rights. All sorts of excuses can be made, and regularly are, but training in being respectful towards adults, and in self-discipline, has to begin at home. Parents are always the greatest influence on their children but the contrast is very noticeable when compared to children on the continent, or in Africa and Asia. In those regions parents insist that their children do as they are told. When children go to school, teachers should just have to teach. Having to train children how to behave should be a secondary and minor part of their task. Certainly there always has to be an element of that, but it should be minimal and not the major consideration that it seems to be today. This is actually impossible to achieve if parents do not back up the teachers. In France, for example, if a child misbehaves continually in school then the parents are called in for discussions and there is still a certain amount of shame attached to this procedure and consequently parents make sure that it does not happen again. In general French children are very well-behaved at school and still have respect for the authority that it represents. This seems to be a disappearing facet of behaviour in Britain to the detriment of the whole community. A good deal of the blame for this situation can be put down to politicians who more and more want to interfere in the day-to-day running of people's lives. The more political interference that there is in the minutiae of living, so the easier it is to blame others for your own shortcomings. It is, or can always be, someone else's fault. Many people, including parents, just fail to take control of their own lives and the minute things start to go wrong, instead of fighting their way out, either demand that the state provides help, or blame it for not helping. There now seem to be counsellors paid for by the taxpayer for just about any eventuality that can ever happen to anyone. Someone has a tongue stuck out at them and the next thing is that they need counselling for their hurt feelings. In many ways it makes a mockery of being an adult and the

109

problem is that these things are self-perpetuating, for the more counsellors there are, the more they seem to be needed.

If you stand back and take a broad look at the whole country it must be said that sub-standard parenting and unpleasant patterns of behaviour are still in the minority. The country still has plenty of very good parents and very good children, but the minority does seem to be on the increase.

RANT 12: ON THE EUROPEAN UNION
AND THE COMMISSION

Is the Commission a democratic body of representatives that we should all wholeheartedly support? The answer, of course, is a resounding NO. The Commission is the real think-tank and powerhouse of the European Union and from it come all the ideas whether good, bad or downright zany that make up the rules and laws of the EU as it now is. When the European Economic Community came into being it was seen as a trading community [at least by the general public across Europe, if not by the founding politicians] and that was it. The idea was good and overall it has been of great benefit to Europe as a whole, as well as its member states. However, with time the Commission has grown in power and as always with power the more the organisation obtains the more it wants. Today the talk is of a federal European state with the Commission at its head and leadership by a President. The members of this all-powerful body are not to be elected by the public which might get it a bit more legitimacy, but are to be nominated by member governments. Those that they have nominated in the past have often tended to be failed politicians in their own countries and governments. It is an easy and generally painless way to get rid of them; nominate them to the Commission where suddenly they have power again, and are able once more to flex their political muscles. They are excessively paid for the work that they do, have exorbitant expense accounts, and overall face very little accountability. Joining the Commission has quite justifiably been called a cushy number and is generally regarded as a 'gravy train' with some validity. The members seem immune from any form of criticism and when this does happen the critics, if they are employed by the Commission, are usually hounded out of their jobs. In the case of one journalist [Hans-Martin Tillack] who exposed a massive fraud in the Eurostat Agency, he was arrested and harried by the police, had all his files confiscated and was taken to court on trumped-up charges. The Commission is ruthless when it comes to protecting its privileges.

The European Parliament, which is elected, is supposed to have ultimate power over the Commission. However, in general it is seen as a toothless body of 'yes' men and women. The MPs are elected, but by an overwhelming minority of the European public. Few people actually know or even care who their Euro representative is, or what he or she does. They are a bunch of total unknowns and the European Parliament does not seem to do a great deal for the overall government of Europe. However, as members of the European Union government they do get lavishly paid and enjoy all the benefits of 'the gravy train'. The EU Parliament once flexed its muscles in 1999 and sacked the whole Commission for being corrupt. It is extremely difficult to imagine just how bad they had become for the Euro Parliament to act. However, this was but a minor crisis in the history of the Commission because the various member states merely re-nominated their own representatives, refusing to admit that they could possibly be corrupt. Hence most of the former Commission members returned to power and the gravy train rolled on. The whole European system of government is seen as a bit of a farce by many, except by those who benefit from its largesse, such as its own members.

One of the biggest criticisms levelled against the Commission is its continual search for standardisation. The aim is to make everything in Europe the same, or at least that is the way many see it. For example, for some inexplicable reason only certain seeds can be sold and those that are not on the list are banned. In pre-EU days there were over 5,000 varieties of potato grown and enjoyed the world over. Any of these could be grown and sold in Britain. Now there are only 427 registered varieties in Britain and it is illegal to sell any of the others. The question is why, what possible harm does it do to the governance of Europe should some enterprising farmer wish to

112

RANT 13: ON BRITAIN AND THE EUROPEAN UNION

Britain has always had a love-hate relationship with the EU. It wants to be a full member and make an important contribution but cannot quite bring itself to be a wholehearted participant. This has a lot to do with the history of Europe, particularly over the past 150 years. Britain has in turn been both great friends, even an ally of the French, and also the worst of enemies. She has also been friends with the Germans who prior to the First World War were actually seen as Britain's natural allies. Immediately after the Second World War there were many suggestions about Britain joining France in an economic treaty of some kind, mainly as a bulwark against the resurgence of Germany. However, at the time it was difficult for politicians to see too far ahead as they were desperately trying to keep their heads above water after such a great cataclysm. The Empire was still basically intact, if crumbling faster than any of our statesmen could see. Also there was always, in the background, the 'special relationship' with America which had always been Britain's biggest trading partner. All these things tended to blinker the politicians of the day and they were all fairly anti-Europe. It should be remembered that the statesmen had been brought up in the shadow of Victorian Britain and this inevitably influenced their thinking. Britain had hitherto been 'great' in every sense of the word. At the beginning of the 20th century Britain had the largest economy in the world. The pound sterling was the world's currency. She had the biggest navy, both merchant and armed. She was undoubtedly the most influential country in the world. Most of the statesmen leading the country after the Second World War still thought we were. None of them wanted to admit that two world wars had actually bankrupted the country. Ideally Britain should have joined the Coal and Steel Community at its outset in 1952 and it may then have had more influence in the affairs of post-war Europe. This would probably have had a beneficial effect on economic recovery. Only when Britain's precarious financial position was admitted by the political classes did they realize that Britain needed Europe rather more than Europe needed Britain. By the time Britain actually joined the Community in 1973 the power structures had already been set in concrete and at the head of these were France and Germany who had actually become great friends. The British felt, as soon as they joined, that they too should be helping to lead. When this failed to happen British sensitivities were somewhat jarred. Furthermore, Britain has had to fight for everything it has ever got from the Community and this inevitably has put her at odds with the top two. Since France and Germany pull the most weight, and have the most influence, they have been able to paint Britain as the trouble-maker and show that she is not ready to be fully integrated into Europe. Actually this is true. Britain, in general, is happy with the trading treaties in Europe but has never wanted greater political integration, and especially not in the form of a federation which appears to be what the Commission and the politicians of the original community countries actually want.

Against this background it is possible to argue that British politicians have worked hard at ways to stop integration coming about. The shock of the 'no' vote against the new constitution both from the French and the Dutch pleased the British no end, for they were sure that when it came to the same thing in Britain the vote would have gone the same way. Had this happened before the French and Dutch votes it would have given the European politicians another stick with which to beat Britain. Hence the 'no' vote resulted in a huge sigh of relief from British politicians, because they did not even have to put the issue to the test. Yet the Commission still has not given up, and they are looking to make some minor changes and resurrect the topic, but there are new member countries which have only just gained independence from the communist yoke and therefore have no intention of giving up any part of their hard-won freedoms so quickly. Looked at from a non-partisan stance it can be argued that the bigger the Union becomes, the harder it will be to achieve any sort of political union. And who has been fighting tooth and nail to enlarge the Union? None other than Britain. France and Germany were not too happy with the latest accession of membership by the eastern European countries but it was pushed through with a great deal of help and lobbying - almost insistence, by Britain. Britain has been the keenest and most persistent advocate of Union enlargement and still wants more members, including Turkey. This is vehemently opposed by quite a number of the original 'Six' and a few of the later members. There are problems with the accession of Turkey, the main one being the question of Cyprus. Until that thorny question is sorted out it is unlikely that Turkey will be allowed to join but it is nevertheless probably only a matter of time. In a referendum carried out on the island, the Turkish community voted for reunification but the Greek populace gave the proposal the thumbs down. However, if they can be converted then there is a very good chance that Turkey will be allowed to join, particularly if Britain has her way. This would probably be the final nail in the coffin of any form of political union in Europe and that would be game, set and match as far as British politicians are concerned.

The government of the EU is already unwieldy, cumbersome in the extreme, creaking at the joints, and needs reforming from top to bottom. About this there is general agreement. It all boils down to a question of 'how'? As far as the British are concerned they want to cut out a lot of the waste, make changes to the Common Agricultural Policy, and to achieve far more efficiency. At the end of the day, however, it has everything to do with trade and nothing to do with politics. The trading part of the Union is the success story within Europe. This has been beneficial to member countries and as

117

a trading colossus it does begin to rival the trading might of the US which in turn is trying to form a similar organisation with the Latin American countries. However, trying to integrate Europe into a political union on the lines of the US is really a non-starter. When the Americans achieved this they had one huge advantage and that was language. The vast majority spoke the same language which made unity a possibility. You feel that this would be the main obstacle to a united Europe. At present there are 23 official languages within Europe and everything has to be translated into these which already makes the governance of the Union a nightmare - quite apart from the millions being paid to battalions of translators and printing businesses. Any suggestion that English should become the official EU language, which would be logical, would instantly be vetoed by the French who already object to so much English being used within the business world in France, and are calling for more French to be spoken instead. Hence it is entirely possible that the idea would collapse at the first hurdle. In any case there are sufficient 'Little Englanders' in Britain to ensure that a political union with Europe never happens.

RANT 14: ON POLARITY IN POLITICS

Polarity of thought has always been a bit of a mystery. People get into a mindset and it seems impossible to change. The best example of this is politics. How often do you hear the words, 'my father was Labour and I always will be' or 'I've been voting Conservative all my life and I'm not changing now'? It seems beyond belief that intelligent, thoughtful people can vote for the same party through thick and thin all their lives. Parties change, ideologies change, and even basic ideas change within politics, and yet people carry on regardless, voting for the same old party. It would seem far more sensible actually to read the various manifestos, boring though they may be, and then to make up your mind each time there is an election. There is actually nothing wrong with voting for a different party each time you vote. Parties are never loyal to their supporters [unless there is a vast donation in the offing] so returning loyalty is rather misplaced. The problem, of course, is that not many people have the time or inclination to read these wonderful political tomes. The other problem is that even if they are read there seem to be few people who believe them. Take the Labour party, for example: who would have thought that back in the days of CND marches and anti-Vietnam war demonstrations, that in 2003 they would lead Britain into a totally unnecessary and unwarranted war in Iraq? Not only that but additionally, they would become real warmongers and persuade parliament, and by all accounts quite a number of the British populace, that little Iraq about 4000 kilometres away was a real threat to Britain. The Conservatives, of course, backed them but that would be expected. The only party that did not support the war were the Liberal Democrats. Will the great voting public remember this very salient point at the next election? Probably not. Again it would not have been credible 30 or 40 years ago to say that a future Labour government could be characterised as being the greatest control freaks in history, and the biggest danger to personal

119

freedoms since King John. The same New Labour leaders who used to march on CND protests in the 70s and 80s are now voting for a new Trident missile system and pushing hard to build a new generation of nuclear power stations. How times have changed, yet core supporters do not seem to see any irony in this. A new nuclear deterrent for Britain is a joke. Instead, just think what that amount of money could do for British infrastructure – paying for new schools, hospitals and trains for the whole country, and still with change left over, yet core supporters will still vote for them.

Another election promise made when New Labour was elected in 1997 was that they would stop the sale of school playgrounds which the Conservatives had started and allowed to continue willy-nilly. Have they kept this pledge? Sales of play grounds have carried on regardless of what was said about the Conservative's policy. Not an important pledge you might say, and easily forgettable at the next election. However, put into the context of obesity and a lack of exercise for children that everyone, including politicians, is complaining about and it becomes, in fact, very important. There are all sorts of new initiatives to get children's weight down and get them to do more exercise, and these inevitably cost the taxpayer, yet it could all have been avoided if every school still had a decent playing field, and the pupils had to play games and do sport as part of the curriculum, as was once the case. Instead the government has been sanctioning the sale of playing fields to developers at the rate of one a week. At this rate there soon will not be any playing fields left. Replacing them with indoor sports facilities is not the same. These usually have to be shared with the public and in any case open fields allow children to career about at will using up their energy, which they cannot do in sports halls. Here, they are constantly supervised, and the uninhibited use of energy is definitely discouraged.

There are, of course, countless other examples of government deceit perhaps some of which are even more important. Nevertheless, just those mentioned here should be enough to make even the most single-minded supporter of the Labour party think twice about voting for them. The same can be said for the Conservative party. There is always a hard core of voters who will not consider changing their allegiance under any circumstances.

RANT 15: ON THE ECONOMY

The economy is a closed-shop to most people. It is, of course, a very complicated subject and as we progress so it becomes more and more complex but it does affect everybody. Capitalism does seem to have an inbuilt destruction button that, when pressed [by the media, or financial pundits, or following rumours amongst the chattering classes], can send the whole pack of cards tumbling for no good reason. A simple example is a company which makes a profit at the end of one year of, say, £250m, in consequence of which its share value instantly increases since it is perceived as being successful and people want to buy its shares. However, the following year it makes only £200m. You would think this remained a reasonable profit and therefore still a good bet, and that all should continue as usual into the following year. But no, a whisper goes round that the company may be in trouble and everybody starts selling their shares and the value of the company falls, and the more it falls the more trouble it is perceived to be in. This selling is often totally irrational, and if, on the other hand, the pundits were to take a closer look then they could judge that a £200m profit was actually quite good, and whilst not quite as high as the previous year was still healthy, which at that level of profit it would be. Why do the commentators and punters imagine that a company's profits will, or even can, increase year-on-year without ever experiencing a dip? Businesses not quoted on the stock market have downturns in their profits and carry on as normal. If a company makes a loss, then that is a different kettle of fish and you can understand a resulting loss in confidence. It is an absolute impossibility for profits to go on up year-on-year *ad infinitum*. It is the same for a country's economy. It cannot sustain growth forever. There has to be a finite level of growth and then there will be contraction, and the more rapid the expansion the greater the contraction. This seems fairly logical but the money markets often are incredibly illogical.

123

A classic example of the havoc that a rumour can cause was 'Black Thursday', October 24, 1929, the day of the great stock market crash on Wall Street. Rumours that some shares were overvalued started a rush on the market and like lemmings the punters scrambled to sell, and sell at any price. All the statements of reassurance from the government and banks that the market remained healthy did nothing to help. This led to massive selling and many share values falling to nil which not only lost a lot of people a lot of money but sent some perfectly good companies into liquidation and set in motion the events that led to the great depression of the 1930s. It is quite extraordinary how perfectly rational businessmen who deal in stocks and shares every day, and many of whom make a good living from it, suddenly can sell because they have heard a rumour, without actually doing an hour's worth of research to find out if actually there is anything wrong with the company in question. The daft thing is that today it still happens when the means of checking are so much easier and faster. The internet has revolutionised communications which means that most of the information that you need is there at the press of a keyboard. Someone sneezes in the Chinese stock market, or someone sees a broker whispering to someone else on Wall Street, and the next thing there is a world-wide panic and shares the world over start falling. Pure lunacy or what?

RANT 16: ON GLOBAL WARMING

Climate change is another fraught subject about which a lot of well-meaning, and even more not so well-meaning, people talk a great deal of hot air. There is no doubt that global weather patterns are changing but then they always have. During their occupation of Britain the Romans were able to grow grapes in England and make wine. In the year 1000 there is ample evidence from archaeological finds to show that the weather in the south of England was equivalent to that of the Loire Valley in France today. Yet by the 14th and 15th centuries the River Thames could freeze to such a thickness that it was possible to hold fairs and light bonfires on the ice during winter. Since then the weather has vacillated but overall has been warming up again. Owing to a lack of instant information in the past no one bothered about it and accepted variable weather as the norm, but today because scientists and people are in instant touch with each other there is much greater awareness of even the tiniest changes. Also, the study of the weather and its patterns is now well advanced and a continuing science of some importance. However, one man's theory is another man's fantasy. So when a scientist formulates a theory then someone or something has to be blamed, and consequently we come up with the concept of man-made global warming. Natural global warming never seems to come into the discussion, yet at a scientists convention at the beginning of 2007, even the scientists, and these were the ones in favour of man-made global warming, said that they were only 80% to 90% sure that man was responsible. If they were really sure they would say 100%, but they are not and 10% to 20% leaves a lot of room for doubt. Furthermore, there are plenty of scientists who doubt this theory altogether [e.g. Professors Paul Layman, Ian Clark, Patrick Michaels, to name but a few], but they are not flavour of the month with the media and the politicians alike so they do not get the same blanket coverage, and often attract no coverage at all.

What the global warming bandwagon has done is to give the politicians an excellent additional excuse to tax people. They can hold their hands up, and they do, and say it is for the good of the planet and the future, and, of course, many people believe them. However, when the chancellor puts a tax on cheap air travel where does that money go? He states that passengers have to pay for their pollution but a reasonable question would be, 'how does this money help to clean anything up, or reduce the CO_2 that has already been emitted into the atmosphere?' The answer is that the cash goes into the chancellor's coffers and nothing gets cleaned because it cannot be. Furthermore, the more tax that he adds the more he will alienate people but actually still do nothing to reduce the number of passengers because here big business is involved and the country relies on big business. It can also be argued that it is a bit of a scandal that people at the lower end of the wage scale should be penalised by having air fares put out of their reach whilst politicians enjoy foreign holidays more often than most, and travel in first-class accommodation on aircraft, which of course, they can afford on their fat payslips. It has also been widely recognised that global shipping produces far more carbon emissions than the aviation industry, yet do you ever hear anyone [from politicians through to the media and the 'Greens'] mention that there ought to be a freeze or reduction in shipping? Big ships use mighty amounts of fossil fuel in their travels around the world [whilst, of course, moving enormous amounts of freight at one time], but the polluting effects are the same. If the government really wanted to lessen carbon emissions it could not do better than to stop any further building of coal-fired power stations and think more in terms of hydroelectricity. This is a more efficient, clean, renewable and less obtrusive method of generating electricity than any other, and yet it never gets a mention. Firms are still being given permission to build coal- and gas- fired power stations which pollute the atmosphere in more ways than one. They use coal which pollutes, and they use foreign coal which has to be transported from as far away as Latin America by very big ships, and guess what they do for pollution? Gas-fired power stations are not much better because their carbon emissions are much the same as for coal and Britain has to import most of its gas leaving the country open to all manner of blackmail. There is enough water in the country to generate all its electricity needs. There may have to be a few dams built and this always 'generates' opposition, but it is still far more climate-friendly than nuclear, coal, gas or even wind-generated power, and yet it never even is considered a possibility. Coming down the ladder a few rungs you find councils charging people who own big cars extra for parking. If anyone thinks this will do anything for global warming, even were it all down to human activity, they are living in cloud-cuckoo land. It is just an extra tax on people but one that the councillors feel they can get away with because people who own big cars are in the minority and generally somewhat unpopular with the rest of the community, largely owing to a touch of jealousy. The same question can be asked of councils: where is that extra money being spent? You can be sure it is not on reducing carbon emissions or extracting carbon from the atmosphere. If councils really want to reduce carbon emissions in their patch, then they should be offering everybody grants to insulate and double-glaze their houses. This would have a far more lasting effect on reducing carbon emissions but entails extra expenditure instead of raising extra revenue, and therefore proves somewhat unpalatable.

On the bottom rung you see the Green Party and ordinary well-meaning members of the public who are sucked in by the very one-sided propaganda. When the experts talk about a person's 'carbon footprint' and follow this by a figure measured in 'tens of tonnes', it does have the effect of frightening people. Not a day goes by when this subject is not brought up by the media in some form or another, and it is not even a drip, drip effect but more like a tidal wave rushing over everyone. Is it any wonder that people come to believe what they cannot stop hearing? If everyone seems to be saying the same thing it will eventually become the truth whether it is, or is not. The Greens would have the country return to the Middle Ages when there were hardly any roads and no industry to speak of, and when global warming was still an unknown phenomenon. Yet it was happening. Could it have been because vast forests were being cut down, and quantities of peat dug up, for household use? Since this was the only form of heating and cooking, massive amounts of wood were burned every day resulting in the partial deforestation of Britain and a great deal of carbon dioxide escaping into the atmosphere. Were the Green Party ever actually to gain power it is hard to see how the country would survive. They would like to reduce carbon emissions down to about nil which would wreck the economy and take it back to the days of the horse and cart, and canal navigation. Ordinary citizens seem quite happy to go along with whatever extra taxes are thrown at them in the belief, because that is what they are told, that they are helping the environment. The same question should be asked – how actually does it help stop carbon emissions? Once the emissions are in the atmosphere they cannot be extracted except by natural means, that is, through absorption by plants and trees. Whilst planting forests of trees would undoubtedly help, councillors and their councils in the vast conurbations of London, Birmingham and the like, do not seem to be rushing forward to spend their ill-gotten gains on such benevolent schemes. If there is one unifying theme to all governments, local and national, and politicians of all hues, it is the need to extract as much money from the people and businesses alike for their treasuries in a way that attracts the least opposition. Now they seem to have found the ideal solution: it is called global warming. It has been hyped to such an extent that it has almost taken over from religion. Sages like Sir David Attenborough talk seriously about it in hushed voices in lectures and TV programmes.

the subject of global warming. The politicians even seemed to 'up the ante' with new and deeper-cutting taxes so that we would all be encouraged to reduce our emissions. Anything said against this scenario is dismissed with contempt, no matter how good the arguments are, for nobody wants to know, particularly the politicians who stand to lose a lot of extra income.

In the US the Oregon Institute of Science and Medicine has a petition, already signed by 31,000 scientists, which insists that carbon dioxide has absolutely no effect on climate whatsoever. In fact, their argument is that CO_2 in the atmosphere is beneficial as it aids plant growth rate. All reviews of the research literature on the subject have turned up not a jot of evidence to support the many claims made of the ill effects of CO_2. There is, of course, a web site and presentation videos to back up their assertions. It seems strange that such an eminent institution can be totally ignored by the politicians.

RANT 17: ON SLAVERY

During the year of the 200th anniversary in 2007 of the abolition of slavery it never ceased to amaze how much hot air was generated specifically by a few who feel that somehow they have personally been wronged. Their forbears may have been but five or six generations down the line to still think that you have a grievance is somewhat over the top. The argument often put forward is that by displacing their ancestors they no longer know their roots, and so there is a gap. First, how many people living in Europe today know their ancestry, or even care? But if this is not an accepted argument then you have only to look at life in most of Africa at that time. Certainly in much of sub-Saharan Africa there was no written word and therefore no records of any sort, making it nigh impossible to trace ancestors. Populations at that time were migratory and the whole family or tribe would move on a regular basis in search of food or trade, or both. In addition slavery existed all over Africa because the in-fighting between families and tribes was endemic, and the ones that lost became slaves.

Second, the Arabs were taking slaves from sub-Saharan Africa as soon as they had conquered the northern fringes. They actually carried on this trade well into the 20th century and not a word is heard about that. Instead, according to the activists, it was all the fault of the Europeans and they are the ones to blame. It is also seldom mentioned that it was actually the Africans themselves who generated the slave trade. The Europeans built the ports from which the slaves were transported, but it was Africans themselves who captured the people and sold them to the Europeans, and there were plenty of African chiefs who became rich on the backs of selling their own people.

Third, there is the question of reparations. The very thought of trying to trace all the descendants of slaves and offering them reparations, well, what a quagmire that would become! It is a bit like a person being held responsible for the crimes of his great-grandfather. There is also the point that not many people in Britain benefited from the slave trade. There were a few rich families, and plenty of nobles and churchmen who took advantage, but the average man in the street 200 years ago was not much better off than a slave in any case, and he certainly had nothing to do with the trade and in no way benefited from it. Yet today his descendants are being asked to pay reparations - somewhat unfairly you might think. Furthermore, the slaves sent to the Caribbean islands now own them. The question may therefore be asked whether they are prepared to compensate the original inhabitants of the islands, who of course, were totally dispossessed of their land. All slavery should and must be abhorred, and as a nation there can be no pride in the past when it comes to slavery. Therefore, the topic should be part of the curriculum in history, and like the Holocaust of the last war it should never be forgotten, but compensation two centuries after its abolition is not really on. On the other hand, it can be argued that there are other forms of 'slavery' that exist even in European society today. This takes on forms very different from the old slavery, but it is slavery nonetheless. The most obvious form is the trafficking in young girls from the East to service the sex trade. This is what should be concentrated upon, rather than giving compensation to people whose great-great-grandfathers were wronged.

RANT 18: ON 'USE-BY' DATES AND FOOD WASTAGE

Whilst it cannot be said that all 'use-by' dates are a waste of time because manifestly they are not, there is a lot that are and these contribute horrendously to food wastage. The obvious examples are products like yoghurt and cheese. Sealed, a tub of yoghurt will last for more than three months after its 'use-by' date without any deterioration whatsoever. Cheeses such as Cheddar and Leicester actually taste better for keeping at least a couple of months after their 'use-by' date. They are usually very immature when packaged and the 'use-by' dates on them are ridiculously short and in reality make no sense at all. The problem is that many young people do not know this and without even a second thought will bin a product if the 'use-by' date has been passed. This, of course, contributes greatly to the amount of food that is thrown out every week which in turn leads to greater need for landfill sites. As these now are reaching full capacity, and according to Government there are no more sites available, so new measures have to be sought. This usually involves extra cost for the public, surprise, surprise. So the government insists on ridiculous 'use-by' dates on food 'to protect the public', and then complains about the amount that is being thrown away. This then leads to extra charges being levied on rubbish collection in an effort to deter waste. It would appear that this is just another easy way to extract more cash from a long suffering public, dressed up, as it usually is these days, in 'greenery'. The best way to go about reducing waste is education and to look again at 'sell-by' and 'use-by' dates that do not actually bear any relationship to the longevity of the product concerned. However, education is the most important issue. Teaching children about food, how to handle it, how to keep it, how to cook it, and most importantly how to tell when it is still good without taking a use-by date as gospel, is pivotal, not only to minimising waste, but to health as well. Teaching youngsters about food may also have the knock-on effect of reducing their dependence on junk food and ready-made meals which would in turn reduce the amount of rubbish. It is a sad fact that so many well-intentioned governmental initiatives are placed on the statute books without being viewed in an overall context. Measures are introduced to sort out a perceived problem and an inspectorate is formed to police it [which they do very efficiently], but often to the detriment of other measures. There is no one to stand back and look at the overall effect that a measure will have on life in general. People in power are always obsessed with building their own little castles and as long as they are following their narrow line of responsibility, they are not bothered what effect it has on other departments. This usually means that governmental departments do not even talk to each other let alone liaise over possible legislation and its overall effects. When 'sell-by' and 'use-by' dates were originally brought in they were seen as, and still are, a very good thing, but no one predicted that they would escalate the amount of good food binned every week along with rubbish. No one saw that people would throw away perfectly good food just because it was past its 'sell-by' or 'use-by' dates. Perhaps a better way of tackling the subject would be to put 'packaged by' and 'sell-by' dates on the goods and educate people to know when food is good and when it is off, because then they could make up their own minds as to whether the food was edible or not. A packaging date offers far more relevant information about a product than does a 'use-by' date dreamt up by some 'food expert'. Of course, the other angle is that the more food we throw away, then the more we need to buy, which in turn means more profit for the manufacturers.

RANT 19: ON THE SANCTITY OF PROPERTY

Possessions are one of the basic human needs. Everybody wants possessions and the more that you have then the more successful you are deemed to be. The ultimate possession is probably property and it seems that most people aspire to own their own property. Again the bigger the property the more successful you are seen to be. During the 18th century the political theorist Edmund Burke put forward the argument that there could be no sustainable economic prosperity and no real meaning to society until the ownership of property was made secure. Looking at societies across the world there does seem to be some truth in this. It happened in Europe a long time ago. When communism gained power in Eastern Europe the government nationalised all property and the vast majority of the population was not allowed to own property. Those societies and their economies did not prosper and in the end the political systems collapsed. In China today the communist party has realised this and in an effort to stave off its own demise has allowed people to buy and hold property securely, and it seems that, to all intents and purposes, China has become a capitalist country with a communist government. However, what a totalitarian government gives it can just as easily take away. Conversely, looking at Cuba, where the populace is still not allowed to own land and where the state hangs on to everything it can, stagnation and underdevelopment are the norm. Communist theory precludes private ownership of property, yet this is exactly what most people want. Evidence of this need was clear in Britain when, in the 80s, council housing was offered for sale to the tenants. Most of those who could, immediately bought their houses. Hence, whilst ownership of property can be seen as normal and even desirable by most people, this is not generally the case with communist governments.

Governments seem to be obsessed with ownership of land. A current and classical case of this is the quarrel between Ethiopia and Eritrea, where these two former friends and allies have fallen out over a couple of square kilometres of land on their shared border. The UN was called in to mediate and both sides agreed to abide by their decision, but when the ruling was given Eritrea did not accept the findings and went to war. This ridiculous little squabble over a useless piece of land that was actually demarcated in the late-19th century when the Italians colonised Eritrea, has so far cost the lives of over 30,000 men, mainly from the Eritrean side. It seems obscene that a leader of a small nation that is already struggling under the yoke of a communist dictatorship should send so many people to their deaths over something so worthless. What drives the leader on to these ends? If it is his personal prestige, then put the question to the country in a vote, and let the people decide. They would undoubtedly say, 'forget it'. All they want is peace and a bit of prosperity. The country suffered 30 years of war before it got its independence, and the people are weary of war and desperately poor, and yet their leader insists on fighting a much bigger neighbour for the sake of a stretch of desert scrubland.

In many ways China is the same except that her goal is a very rich island. The logic, however, is the same. China is a country of 9.5 million square kilometres and a population of 1.2 billion people, and yet it wants more. It lays claim to Taiwan which was once part of China but broke away during the communist takeover and has been a very successful capitalist country ever since. Put to the vote, there is no doubt that the people of Taiwan would vote to stay independent. But China sabre-rattles on a constant basis stating that it is a province of China and should submit to its rule. China is big enough, prosperous enough, and has enough of its own problems, to be able to ignore Taiwan altogether, yet it cannot.

Argentina and the Falkland Islands provide another example. The Falkland Islands are about 800 kilometres from Argentina. They are fairly barren and have a population of barely 2000 all of whom speak English and trace their ancestry to Britain. They want to remain British and yet the Argentinians went to war with Britain over them, lost the war plus many hundreds of men, and all for what? There are supposedly mineral resources surrounding the islands, plus, of course, the fishing rights, but are these worth losing lives over? On the other hand, had the Argentinians negotiated quietly instead of sending in the army the Falklands would probably have been theirs by now, as in reality Britain sees them as a bit of a nuisance and a drain on the economy. As there is no loyalty from governments they would have negotiated irrespective of what the locals wanted. However, now it is a point of principle which the government cannot ignore. In the past, and had there been no war, public opinion could have been overridden, or just ignored, for it would not have been very vociferous because not many people had even heard of the Falklands. Now there would be a massive outcry, particularly from those who fought, and from the relatives of those who died. Any government trying to hand the Falklands to Argentina today would face stiff resistance.

RANT 20: ON THE DIFFERENCE BETWEEN 'RIP-OFF' BRITAIN AND 'PEOPLE- FRIENDLY' FRANCE

Here in conclusion, and having made many criticisms of Britain today, it may be appropriate to compare us with another country which seems to go out of its way to help people, rather than to hinder them. France is the nearest foreign country to Britain and in many ways is quite similar. Both are European, both members of the EU, both democracies, both were allied during the last two world wars, the economies are largely similar, and since the Norman invasion in 1066, and the Huguenot refugee crises of the 1500 and 1600s when thousands of French Protestants arrived in England, there has been a fair bit of French blood flowing through British veins. Yet the differences between the two countries are palpable. In general, people in France are friendlier, the countryside is better kept, towns and villages are cleaner, and service, be it in a shop or restaurant, is more attentive. The general attitude and feeling of well-being compares with that experienced in Britain during the 1950s.

The first thing that comes to mind is the intrusiveness of authority in Britain where there are more cameras per person than in communist China. In France there are hardly any and certainly none in what might be termed reasonably-sized towns and villages. They are not needed in France; the people do not like them and in all probability would not stand for them. It would also be very difficult for local authorities to introduce CCTVs in the stealthy and underhand way that they have done in Britain. At the first sign of anything like that there would be a queue outside the mayor's office demanding to know what was going on. They do not even like speed cameras for which a good argument can always be made. But even here a difference exists between the two countries. In the case of static speed cameras in France there is always a large warning sign

139

about 200 or 300 metres before each camera. Furthermore, on sale [and even in little advertising freebies] you can obtain a map that indicates every camera in France. When police use radar traps, they have to publish in the local press on which roads they are going to be and often the local radio station will announce where they will be that day. If this is not more people-friendly than Britain, what is?

Buying a house is always a traumatic experience and in England it seems to get worse as the years go by. You can make an offer, have everything accepted and agreed, only to find the buyer can pull out on the day of completion without any redress or compensation. By this time the vendor may have spent a lot of money and probably has the furniture removers standing by, or even fully loaded. This is really a very unsatisfactory situation, if not pure madness. In France once a price has been agreed a legal contract is signed and a 10% deposit paid. Should the buyer withdraw, then the deposit is lost. Nor can the vendor pull out because the law would compel him to sell on the basis of the binding contract. Hence there is no gazumping, or withdrawing before completion. The 'solicitor' in charge, in France called the *notaire*, has a fixed fee no matter how much work goes into the conveyance. Their fees are fixed by government, and at the end of the sale a full breakdown of where these fees have gone is given in the form of a receipt. Not only that, but there is often a small refund as the fixed fee is the maximum that can be charged. Normally the same *notaire* acts for both parties [as they are semi-government officials] and have to give impartial advice. However, should one party wish to appoint his own *notaire* he can and the overall fees remain the same – the *notaires* have to split the fee. The surveys completed for a house are intended to ascertain whether there is any asbestos, lead or termite pollution, and there is also a calorific survey to see how well the house is insulated. These then remain in force in the case of lead, for life, in the case of asbestos for two years, and the remaining two for twelve

140

months each, so that paying a survey fee is not required every time an offer is made. Consequently, buying a house in France, particularly for a foreigner, is a lot easier and far less stressful by the rules that govern the process, and these are, for the most part, adhered to strictly.

The government also tries to keep down the price of housing so that it is affordable for everyone. One of the ways this is achieved is by having a limit on the profit to be made through speculation. So should a property be bought and then sold on, purely for speculative purposes, the maximum profit that can be made is seven-twelfths of the buying price. If a larger sum is made then the authorities have the right to confiscate the difference and return it to the original owner. This may seem like a restriction of trade etc., but at least people can afford to buy a house which is more than can be said for many people in Britain! The government also runs a scheme for French first-time buyers by which a youngster who has rented a house for two years, and can prove that he has not defaulted on the rent, can then request a loan and the government will give him a 100% mortgage at 0% interest.

Profits on the sale of a second home are also quite highly-taxed; in the case of a resident in France the tax is 26% of the profit and 16% for a non-resident. This is the case for the first five years of ownership and then on a reducing scale over the next ten at which point it drops to zero. There is also a sanction available to the mayors of towns and villages, insofar that should they want, they have the right to pre-empt any house purchase in their area. So if an outsider came along and wanted to buy a house, put in an offer and it was accepted, then the deal first has to go before the mayor. If he thinks too many houses are being sold as second homes, then he has the right to buy it for the price accepted, and it can be sold on to a local. This means that villages can ensure they never become second home or dormitory settlements where inevitably trade and most

141

other activities disappear. This is called looking after your constituents.

A further consideration is planning permission. What you do inside your own house is your own business and does not need planning permission. If the living area is being increased, as in a loft conversion, for example, the authorities want to know so they may increase the rates, but they do not always do this. Here you fill in a relatively simple form and submit it to the *Mairie*, but they do not stop you doing it. Altering the exterior in any way requires full planning permission. If this is a fairly simple change then the applicant can complete the whole process himself, and since the forms and other requirements are fairly simple, it is easy to do and no cost is involved. Once submitted, it may be returned with some changes requested or suggested, but if you have been sensible and, in advance, asked the local mayor for advice, then it will go through smoothly. Even if it does come back, when the amendments are made it quickly will be passed. When it returns finally with the stamp of approval, usually within a few weeks, and they do not charge you a cent. In contrast, obtaining planning permission in Britain is seen often as a nightmare by the average person who usually has to call in experts who are expensive. It seems as though the planning departments are there in order to harass and harry applicants in every way and, finally, when permission is granted they lumber the applicant with a big bill that adds to the cost of the project.

Rates, or Council Taxes, are another point of contention. These taxes in Britain are extortionate. You can only surmise whether councils and local government in general are incredibly inefficient, or if there is a great deal of corruption. Britain certainly has a lot of grossly overpaid people in local government. It seems obscene that in Tower Hamlets in London, hardly a wealthy area, there were nine council employees in 2007 earning over £100,000 a year. Does anyone ever question what these people actually do for their money?

142

In London boroughs alone there are 194 people who are paid more than £100k annually and overall in England some 500 staff in local government who receive more than this sum. Mention this to a local government officer in France and you get whistles of total disbelief mixed with a lot of Gallic huffing and puffing. These are extraordinary salaries and they do not really match the job responsibilities. In France they go out of their way to keep rates down to the barest minimum and yet they manage to provide as good if not better services than most in the UK. The mayoral form of government in France works well. The mayor has the power, is usually well-known to his constituents, does not take freebies on the rates, and in fact gets a very small stipend. Above all, the mayor is up for re-election every seven years so should he not get it right he is voted out. In most places the post is part-time and the mayor has to rely on his day job for a living, so helping to keep the rates low. In Britain the authorities are currently looking for ways to increase communal taxes, for example by charging for everyone's view, which is, in all honesty, risible were it not so monstrous, but it could happen. In France they prefer to look for ways to reduce the rates.

One of the greatest differences between the two countries lies in the attitude of local government towards the individual. In Britain it is very difficult to get past a receptionist to see anyone in authority, or to have a complaint sorted out. It really is impossible by telephone so a visit to the town hall seems to be the only remedy. However, on arrival the problems begin. Actually seeing anyone face-to-face is purposely made difficult and all the best efforts usually lead to frustration. In France, despite their reputation for bureaucracy, it is still easy to see the person in charge for the relevant problem area. Then when he is seen, he will go out of his way to sort things out. Although somewhat cumbersome, French local government is approachable and seems to want to help and usually has a friendly face. Another big bonus is that most local government services in

France are free, because that is what the rates are for! In Britain most, if not all, services have to be paid for as an extra, and you are left wondering where all the tax money goes! How can France give such good service on so little and Britain give so little service at such a high cost? By way of a small comparison, a little village in the French equivalent of rural Yorkshire provides mains drains, street lights, rubbish collection once a week from wheely bins, is swept regularly, has flowers planted in the summer, and generally is well-maintained. For a three-bedroom terrace cottage with a good garden and garage and on all the 'mains', the rates are about £350 pa. A similar property in a Yorkshire village with similar services would cost in excess of £1000 pa., depending, of course, on which tax band the house is in. In France these iniquitous bands do not exist, although it remains a bit of a mystery exactly how they compute the taxes, but they do keep them low. An example of band charges in an area in Yorkshire [supplied by the County Council] starts at the lowest, which is property valued at up to £40k [if such an animal still exists], which is band A, and the tax is about £900. Band D is property valued at between £68 and 88k, for which the taxes are about £1350 a year. The top band, H, is property valued at £320k and over, and the tax is £2251. The valuations were made in 1991 and are the latest the council had. As the value of property has risen considerably since then it is probable that there will be a revaluation in the near future and a concomitant rise in taxes. These are the type of figures that you might expect in the centre of Paris, but not out in the sticks.

Parking is another area of great contrast. All villages in France provide ample free parking as do a lot of the major towns. Where they do charge it is reasonably priced, in a town centre for instance, at one euro an hour. In main TGV stations it is a maximum of five euros per day and in some places as little as ten euros per week. Compare these costs with those charged in Britain where some population. In France, major dates such as Armistice Day [November 11], Victory in Europe Day [May 8], Bastille Day [July 14] are each marked by placing the Tricolour around every war memorial in the country. For the war commemorations there will often be a small parade of veterans followed by a church service. On Bastille Day, towns and villages put on fetes, pageants and usually a wonderful firework display at night. The smaller towns and many villages are also great at organising interesting events that pull in the crowds and which also give the locals a wonderful feeling of togetherness. These events can be as disparate as something connected to local history, and in which the people all participate by dressing up, to a simple pig roast followed by a dance. A very small and quiet little village had eight births in one year. This was so exceptional that the local mayoress organised for eight oak trees [of the evergreen variety] to be planted in the little park in the centre of the village. On the day, the supplier attended in order to demonstrate how they should be planted and the whole village turned out to watch. The local senator was also present and after the planting, which each family undertook for itself, there followed coffee and biscuits in the community hall, all paid for by the village. It is such attention to detail that gives the French their feeling of togetherness and solidarity. Any foreigners present are made to feel totally welcome and part of the community.

Family ties are far more important to people in France than is the case in Britain. Children and grandchildren visit their parents and grandparents on a regular basis and always seem to enjoy these visits. It never comes across as a chore. On Mother's Day, in particular, families expect to get together and have a party always accompanied by plenty of flowers for mum. Even in the case of the departed, graves are visited regularly and flowers placed. On All Saints Day every cemetery in the country will have crowds of visiting people and again flowers are placed on graves, typically chrysanthemums. The French are a lot more tactile than the British. When people meet friends or acquaintances they always shake hands and male and female friends will always kiss on the cheek. Children up to the age of about ten are expected to kiss the adult friends of their parents when they meet. These things go a long way to making the whole society friendly, more cohesive and definitely more laid-back than is the case in Britain.

Tied-in with the above is the lack of a yob culture throughout France. French youths never go out with the intention of getting plastered or looking for a fight in the evenings. In Britain you can find this behaviour thriving not only in the big cities but in rural areas too. You can see graffiti and vandalism throughout the country, whether in big cities, towns or small villages. Along with this is the 'lager-lout' culture that gets British youth such a bad name both at home and abroad. This does not happen in France. There are occasions when French youngsters get a bit tipsy but this always seems to be tied-in with a special occasion. They may get a bit loud but it never seems to end in any sort of violence or yobbish behaviour, and very seldom do girls get involved.

One of the great traits of the French is their total lack of awe for authority. If the government says it is going to do something with which the majority disagrees, then the people react. This usually means bringing the country to a juddering halt but they do get listened to and the government of the day knows it has a fight on its hands. Nine times out of ten it is the government that gives way to the overwhelming popular clamour. The last time this happened in Britain was the tanker driver's protest a few years ago that nearly brought the country to a standstill. The government was in a flat spin and promised to respond to their grievances in order to get them back to work. When all had quietened down they brought in legislation banning such a re-occurrence and the great British public, having been almost in a state of euphoria at the driver's cheek at

147

rattling the government, sat back and did nothing. This is probably why France does not have intrusive cameras on every street corner, nor a 'jobsworth' around every bend telling people what they can and cannot do, and why the numbing culture of political correctness that now exists in the UK does not in France. In short, France is not the 'nanny state' that Britain has become, and visitors to France experience and enjoy an almost tangible difference the minute that they arrive in the country.

CONCLUDING REMARKS

In conclusion, there are plenty of things to be grumpy about but while some are fairly trivial there are some that should at least give rise to concern. The most important of these is probably the continual erosion of personal liberty. There are investigative journalists and others who try and expose this creeping loss of freedom. They write articles in the press and publish books about it, yet there appears to be no sign of alarm from the general public. The big question is why? This insidious growth of state power is truly Machiavellian, for when asked, any politician in Parliament today will deny that it is happening, yet the evidence is stark. In the 50s there were fewer than ten reasons why the state could legally enter a private house without the owner's permission. Today, according to the Centre for Policy Studies, there are 266 reasons why officers of the government can enter your house without permission. If this is not a cause for concern, what is? One of the big problems here is that you feel somewhat helpless when confronted with the might of state power. Politicians, who are the guilty parties, can look you straight in the eye and swear it is not true and that the problem is being exaggerated. The other thing is that there is no political party which admits it is happening or will make a manifesto pledge to stop it because, if there were, then at least the public could make its vote count for something. The last 15 or so years have been a disaster for personal freedoms. There have been about 3000 new criminal offences added to the statute book, many of which are so trivial that you wonder how such busy people as MPs find the time to be distracted by such trifles. Britain is not becoming a 'nanny state'- it already is one! The danger is that we are becoming a police state, too....